Eric Giguère

Make Easy Money with Google

Using the AdSense Advertising Program

Peachpit
Press

Make Easy Money with Google:
Using the AdSense Advertising Program
Eric Giguère

Peachpit Press is a division of Pearson Technology Group.

Peachpit
1249 Eighth Street
Berkeley, CA 94710
510/524-2178
800/283-9444
510/524-2221 (fax)
Find us on the World Wide Web at: www.peachpit.com

To report errors, please send a note to errata@peachpit.com

Peachpit is a division of Pearson Education

Project editor: Cheryl England
Developmental editor: Steve Anzovin
Production editor: Lupe Edgar
Copy editor: Janet Podell
Compositor: Maureen Forys, Happenstance Type-O-Rama
Indexer: Karin Arrigoni
Cover design: Mimi Heft
Cover photos: Chloe © Scott Cowlin, .Thought blog © Jeff Carlson; all others © Getty Images, Inc.
Interior design: Maureen Forys, Happenstance Type-O-Rama

ISBN 0-321-32114-6

9 8 7 6 5 4 3 2 1

Printed and bound in the United States of America

Dedication

For Jean-Claude, always eager to learn and explore.

Acknowledgements

The book-writing process is such an individually oriented task that it's easy to forget that there are others involved. I'd like to take this opportunity to thank the people who've helped get this book off the ground. First, of course, are Lisa and Victoria, who put up with some long hours on my part. Especially little Victoria, who often wondered why I was spending so much time in front of my computer. Then there are the early reviewers, who gave of their time to look over what I'd written: Jean-Claude Giguère, Anik Giguère-Biollo, Robert Kao, John Gilhuly, and especially C. Enrique Ortiz. My agent, Carole McClendon at Waterside Productions, was excited to read a book of mine she could truly understand. Finally, there are the Peachpit people to thank: Cheryl England, the patient and prodding editor who liked my pitch for this book; Steve Anzovin and Janet Podell, for developing and copyediting it; and of course all the others involved in getting it into its final printed form.

About the Author

Eric Giguère has been a Web devotee since the early 1990s, watching as it evolved into an intricate yet everyday tool used by millions to inform, socialize, and even make money. The author of several books, including *Java 2 Micro Edition* and *Palm Database Programming*, Eric has also written hundreds of magazine articles on Web applications, programming, and Java. His first articles were written when he was 14, back in the days when he was programming Commodore VIC-20 computers for fun.

Eric's formal training consists of undergraduate and graduate university degrees in computer science and more than 15 years of hands-on programming experience. He has held senior software development positions at Sybase and iAnywhere Solutions, a Sybase subsidiary that develops mobile database, security, and middleware solutions—and, Eric claims, one of the best places to work in Canada. You can find out more about Eric at www.ericgiguere.com or send him questions at ericgiguere@ericgiguere.com.

Contents

Introduction

Sometimes it's the small events that are the most exciting. Like the day I made three cents. Not three dollars. Not thirty dollars. Just three cents. And yet it was a *very* exciting event because of what those three cents represented.

I made those three cents the first time someone clicked an advertisement on one of my Web pages. And it was just the beginning. Every time an ad was clicked, I'd make money. The more visitors I had, the more money I'd make. The pages that I had created purely out of interest and paid for out of my own pocket could pay for themselves, or possibly even turn a profit. *That's* what was so exciting about those three cents.

The great thing was that it was really easy, because Google was doing all the hard work for me, through their free AdSense program. All I had to do was give them space on my pages to display the ads. They chose the ads, tracked the clicks, and charged the advertisers. Even better, they analyzed my pages and selected ads that were relevant to the topic of each page. All I had to do was keep my pages updated and do my best to attract a steady stream of visitors, which I was already doing. The truth was, *anyone* could do what I was doing!

Just as exciting was the day a few months later when the first check from Google arrived in my mailbox. It was a small check, but it was real. I almost framed it instead of cashing it!

That's what this book is all about—the excitement of making money with Google without having to be a computer expert. You'll need some Web pages, but I'll show you how to build those. Don't worry, there's no programming required! All you need is a computer and a connection to the Internet.

Can It Really Be Done by Anyone?

You're skeptical. Maybe you're thinking, "This author is an experienced writer and an experienced Web page and application developer, so of course to him it all seems very simple." While there's no denying that having a background like mine helps, it's definitely *not* a requirement. Making money with Google is easy to do with the right guidance. The concepts are not hard and can be mastered by anyone with the patience to learn them. Kind of like most things, really.

I think what scares most people about computers and the Web is the terminology involved, not the concepts. I'll be the first to admit that technical people use a *lot* of buzzwords and obscure terms when they're talking about technology. It really *is* a specialized vocabulary. But specialized vocabularies aren't unique to the computer industry. Look at medicine: Doctors talk to one another in technical terms that the average person doesn't understand. This is good; specialized vocabularies are concise and more precise than general, everyday vocabularies. They can make communication quicker and more accurate—as long as *all* parties to the communication speak the same language.

What if you *don't* understand the language? That's where technical people often come up short compared to medical personnel. Doctors and nurses learn to talk to their patients using terms the patients can understand. Many techies don't learn this skill, which is why technology can seem so foreign and unapproachable to nontechies. But there *are* people like me who can bridge the gap and write books like this one.

Please understand that there are no secrets in this book: Like many things, everything discussed here is already described somewhere on the Web—you just have to find it and understand it. Not only do I save you the hassle of finding the material, I also make sure you understand it. That's the primary value of this book.

Is This the Book for You?

If you're reading this book because you've read one of my previous works, be aware that this book is something of a departure for me. My previous books have all been programming books. This book is different, because it's written for the average computer *user,* not the average computer *programmer*—people like my wife or my father, not my co-workers. If you're looking for a technically oriented book, you're reading the wrong book—you can safely put the book back on the shelf and keep browsing.

The rest of you are about to begin an interesting journey, because *Make Easy Money with Google* is as much about understanding the Web as it is about making money on the Web. The Web may seem mysterious to you now, but it's built on simple (yet powerful) foundations. It's a tool for finding and sharing information, and that's exactly how you'll make your money.

The book is written as a narrative, which is not the typical format for a "computer" or "digital lifestyle" book. Though the stories are fictional, the characters you'll encounter are composites of people I've interacted with before. They all have nontechnical backgrounds, and you should relate to them quite easily. The light, conversational style will, I hope, make the book a pleasure to read.

Please note that I didn't title this book *Make Oodles and Oodles of Money with Google*. I'm sure there are people who make lots of money using the techniques I describe, but I'd be lying to you if I said this book is going to make you rich. *I'm* not rich. But I *have* made money with Google, and so can you. And you can have fun doing it!

How to Use This Book

Before we get started with our adventure, here's some important information about using this book—the resources you'll need to gather, descriptions of each chapter, and information about the companion Web sites.

Resources You'll Need

As I've already said, this is a book for nontechnical people. If you can surf the Web, you can understand this book. The only resources you'll need are these:

- ▶ **A computer.** Regular access to a computer is essential. Not only do you need a place where you can sit and create your Web pages, you'll want to have a copy of the pages stored locally for safekeeping and for testing. The operating system doesn't matter, though the examples and software discussed in this book are for Windows XP or Macintosh OS X only.

- ▶ **A high-speed Internet connection.** This should be a given, but it's worth mentioning. You can still build and maintain your Web site using a slow-speed dial-up connection, but a faster connection is *so* much more pleasurable.

- ▶ **A credit card.** You'll need a way to pay for some expenses. There aren't many, and they're not large expenses, but a credit card is the easiest way to pay for them.

What you *don't* need to do is buy high-priced software to help you build Web pages. There's enough free software available on the Internet to make those kinds of purchases unnecessary. We'll be looking at some of this free software later in the book.

Chapter Descriptions

As a narrative, this book is meant to be read sequentially, so please follow the chapters in the order in which they're presented:

1. **Making Money with Google.** Introduces the four-step process for making money with Google and reviews important concepts like Web sites, Web servers, and blogs.

2. **Understanding AdSense.** Describes Google's AdSense program: what it is, how it works, and how to join the program. Also discusses why advertising is so important to the Web.

3. **Finding Something to Say.** Lists techniques for choosing page topics and building content that attracts visitors.

4. **Getting Ready to Say It.** Explains how to register a good name for your site and find a hosting service.

5. **Designing Your Site.** Discusses how to design your site: choosing a look and feel, handling site navigation issues, and making the site attractive to humans *and* Google.

6. **Building Your Site.** Shows how to build Web pages from scratch using HTML and CSS—don't worry, it's *not* programming—and how to ensure that viewers see the site you want them to see.

7. **Becoming an AdSense Publisher.** Describes how to become an AdSense publisher, how to manage your AdSense account, and how and when you can expect to be paid.

8. **Publishing Ads on Your Site.** Discusses the different ad formats and how to track page performance. Also lists tips and tricks for making effective use of AdSense.

9. **Making Money from Your Site.** Explains how to drive traffic to your site and how to optimize your pages to get better clickthrough rates and better-paying ads.

10. **Expanding Your Horizons.** Wraps things up with a brief discussion of affiliate and referral programs.

As you can see, there's a deliberate progression that takes you from learning the basic concepts to building your site to making money with the site.

Companion Web Sites

Not only have you purchased a great book, you also get access to four great Web sites, including www,MakeEasyMoneyWith-Google.com, the official companion site for this book. On the companion site you'll find additional information that updates or enriches the material you're reading. The other sites are example sites built to complement the narrative. You can register yourself with the main site to download your own copies of the other sites for use as additional study material.

The companion site can also be accessed using the short form www.memwg.com, an unremarkable name derived from the initial letters of each word in the book's title. Within the book, links to the companion site always use this shorter form to save you finger strain and to avoid difficulties in typesetting the text.

And as a bonus, registered readers who build Web pages using this book can also apply for a link from the companion site back to their pages, with no strings attached. This is an easy way to get some extra traffic to those pages. (See www.memwg.com/free-listing for the full details, but please note that I reserve the right *not* to link to inappropriate or otherwise unsuitable pages.)

Let's Get Ready

It's time to start our narrative. If you don't already have a computer and a high-speed Internet connection, now would be a great time to get yourself set up. In the meantime, let's begin the story.

section one

Starting

Content

Design

AdSense

Traffic

chapter one

Making Money with Google

> Claude: Is it easy to build a Web site?

> Eric: Sure. You can find instructions on the Web. There are lots of books about building Web sites, too.

> Claude: But can you make money with a Web site?

> Eric: Absolutely. And you don't even need anything to sell. I do it with my own site.

Claude was visiting me one day. As an early retiree with two grown children, Claude has a lot of free time, and he spends a good chunk of it at his computer, talking to friends and acquaintances and trying all kinds of software. He isn't technical, but he's an expert computer user—he knows the applications he uses regularly far better than I do. He likes to buy electronic gadgets and computer accessories. When he has questions, though, he calls me up for help.

On this day, we were talking about Web pages and Web sites. "Is it easy to build a Web site?" he asked me.

"Sure," I said, "you can find instructions on the Web. There are lots of books about building Web sites, too." I offered to lend him some of the books I had.

"But can you make *money* with a Web site?" he shot back. Now we were getting to what he really wanted to know.

"Absolutely," I said. "And you don't even need anything to sell. I do it with my own site." Which was the truth.

"Is that why you have ads on your pages?" he wondered. (If you go to **www.EricGiguere.com**, you'll see text ads on the right side of most pages. See **Figure 1.1**).

"That's how I make money with my site," I agreed. Now I knew what he wanted, but he was probably afraid to ask the obvious question: *Can I do it, too?*

The Elevator Pitch

It was time for my elevator pitch about making money with Google. Maybe you're unfamiliar with the term *elevator pitch*. An elevator pitch is a very short talk or presentation designed to drum up interest in an idea or concept. It traditionally refers to an on-the-spot idea description made by an entrepreneur to grab the attention of a potential investor cornered in an elevator. We weren't in an elevator, but I wanted to grab Claude's attention.

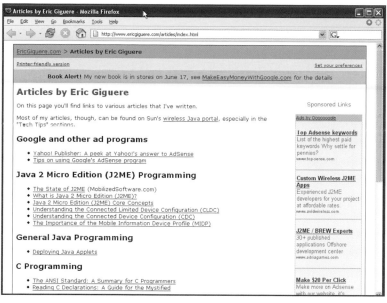

Figure 1.1 The EricGiguere.com Web site.

"Claude," I pitched, "anyone can make money with Google using a four-step process with no programming required. If you can surf the Web, you can learn the process."

He was interested. "What's the catch? Do I have to buy one of those get-rich-quick systems?"

"No," I said, "there's no 'system' to buy, and only a few small expenses." And then a caution on my part: "I can't *guarantee* that you'll make money by following the process, but the chances are good that you'll make *some* money."

"*Some* money's better than *no* money," Claude said, and I had to agree.

The Four Steps

Since Claude seemed eager to continue, I sat down next to him and sketched the process for him on a pad of paper. "Like most things,"

Web Stats

Many sites offer statistics on Internet usage; a site that covers worldwide Internet usage patterns and trends is www. internetworldstats.com/.

I explained, "the amount of money you make will probably be in direct proportion to the amount of thought and effort you put into the process." Here are the steps I described to Claude.

Step 1: Create Some Web Pages

The first step is to create some Web pages. Don't look so dubious—Web page creation is not as mysterious as it seems. The basics are easy to understand, and there are many tools (both free and commercial) available to help you. What's hard is coming up with the *content* for those pages.

When you think about it, the Web is all about content—surfing the Web is just looking for stuff. With billions of pages out there, the competition for a surfer's attention is very stiff. The better your content, the more unique and useful it is, the better your chances that others will find it. That's why I'll be discussing creating good content—finding something to say and saying it well—before getting into the mechanics of actually creating Web pages.

Step 2: Show Ads on the Pages

The second step is to show ads on those Web pages. Viewing Web pages doesn't usually cost the reader anything. Few sites can get away with charging for access to their material—there's simply too much competing material already freely available on the Web.

If you can't charge for access to the material, how do you make money? It depends on the nature of your pages. If you're running a business that sells products or services, then the pages are indirect moneymakers. They're a marketing expense, a cost of doing business. But you don't have anything to sell. Or do you?

Well, actually, you do—you have space on your Web site. You can make money by selling parts of your Web pages as advertising space.

This is the same way that newspapers and magazines—the classic pre-Web content services—make most of their money.

Google makes this step easy. Once you've created your Web pages—or at least some of them—you join Google's AdSense program. Google will read the pages you made, analyze the content that's on them, and use that analysis to select ads that are relevant to the content of the page. All you need to do is insert some Google-supplied code—don't worry, there's no programming involved, just cutting and pasting—into the pages. If someone clicks an ad on one of your pages, Google gives you a cut of the per-click fee they charge advertisers. And it's all automated, even the ad selection (**Figure 1.2**).

Step 3: Drive Traffic to the Pages

The third step is to increase the number of visitors, or *traffic*, to your pages. Just showing ads isn't enough: in most cases, you only make money when visitors click on the ads, and the ads will be clicked by only a small percentage of your page visitors. Increase the number of visitors, and you'll increase the number of clicks.

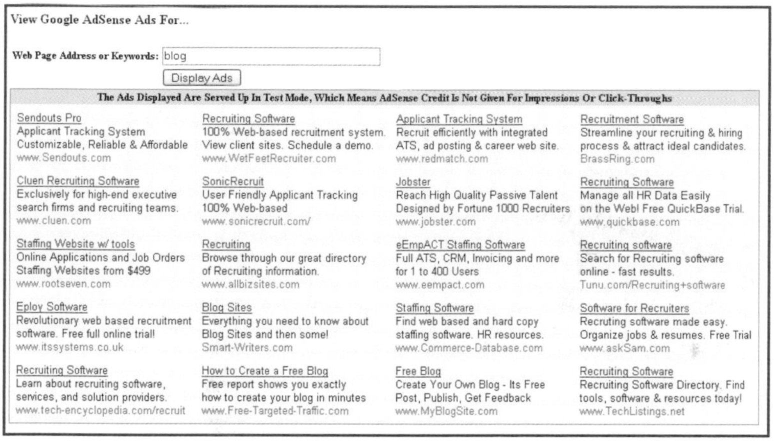

Sample AdSense Ads

If you'd like to see sample AdSense ads based on any URL or keyword, try Digital Point Solution's handy Sandbox utility at www.digitalpoint.com/tools/adsense-sandbox/.

Figure 1.2 Sample AdSense ads generated by Digital Point Solution's Sandbox tool.

Find Your Rank

Google rankings are available at www .googlerankings.com/.

> ## Why AdSense?
>
> While it's true that AdSense is just one advertising system, it offers a number of advantages over most of the others. Not only is there no cost to join it, it's also available to almost anyone with content on the Web. The ads are primarily text-based (image-based ads are also available as an option) and come in a wide variety of formats for placement on your pages. The ads are also drawn from the same large pool of advertisements shown by Google on its own search pages. Finally, the automated page analysis ensures that the ads displayed on your pages are relevant to the content of those pages.

This step sounds simple, but it's not. In fact, driving traffic to your pages is the hardest step of the process. With so many Web pages out there, the chances that someone will stumble upon yours by accident are small. Your best bets for traffic are to generate good word of mouth and to get your pages higher in Google's page rankings (**Figure 1.3**).

Step 4: Monitor and Update the Pages

The final step is to monitor and update your Web pages on a regular basis. This is the easiest step to perform, but it's an important one—you want your visitors to keep coming back. If they see that your pages are current, that the content changes in regular and interesting ways, they're more likely to come back. You want them to come back. You want them to link to your pages from their own pages. You want them to tell others about your pages. Making sure your pages are always available and are always up-to-date will make this possible.

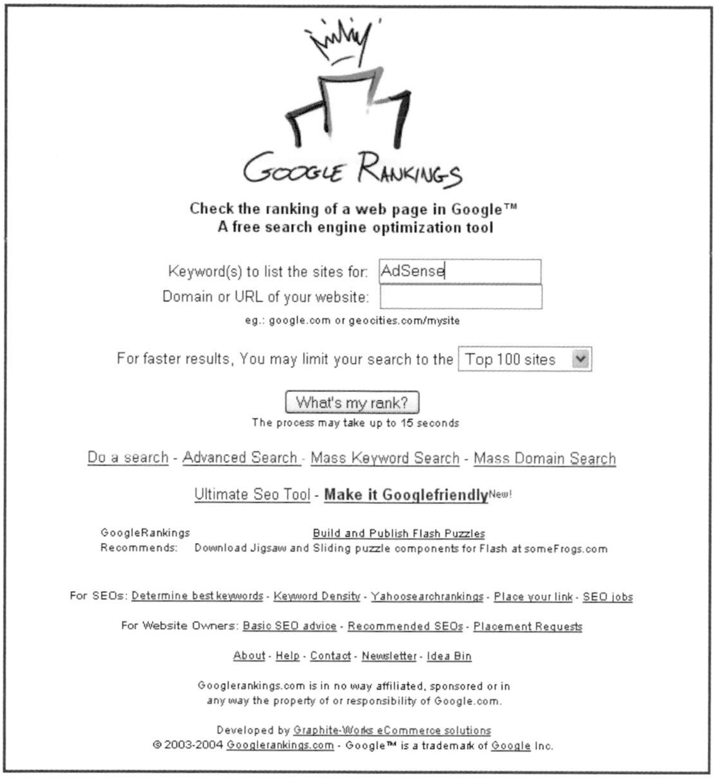

Figure 1.3 Google page rankings.

Monitoring your pages can also help you create new content. With a bit of work, you can usually figure out which search terms visitors are using to find your site. These terms—and some of them may surprise you—will suggest topics to focus on when creating new pages or updating existing pages.

Who Cares about My Pages?

After I had described the process, Claude expressed doubts about it. "I don't know," he said. "It seems too easy. I can see why popular sites like `CNN.com` and `Forbes.com` make money by selling advertising space, but why would any advertiser want to rent space on *my* pages?"

About AdWords

See Chapter 2 for more on Google's AdWords program.

Claude's question wasn't unreasonable. Why *would* an advertiser deal with anyone other than the big sites? There are a few good reasons, in fact:

▸ Not everyone visits the big sites.

▸ The big sites are expensive advertising venues.

▸ Ads on big sites are aimed at broad demographic segments.

But no advertiser can afford to place ads on millions of small Web sites—it's just too much work. Even dealing with the big sites is a hassle. That's why advertisers use advertising services like Google's AdWords or Yahoo!'s Overture.

"It's all about finding the right audience," I explained to Claude. "If your pages attract a segment of the population that advertisers want to target, even if it's a small segment, they'll be interested. But they want the advertising service to find that segment for them. That's where Google's AdSense program comes in."

Perhaps an analogy would help my case. "Look at the economy," I continued. "There are many more small businesses than big businesses, but big business gets all the press and publicity. Yet small businesses employ as many people as big businesses and account for most of the long-term job gains, according to government statistics. You don't have to be big to make a difference. Most sites on the Web are small. That doesn't make them unimportant or uninteresting."

A Case in Point

Claude was still dubious. "So how much money can I make?" he asked me. "I bet it's not much."

"It depends on two factors," I answered. "How many visitors does your site get? How much are the advertisers willing to pay you? Multiply the two together and you'll know how much money you'll make."

Claude was direct: "So how much money do you make?"

I was expecting this question. "It varies from month to month, really. When I first displayed the ads, I made on average less than a dollar every day. Some days it was just a few cents, some days it was over a dollar."

He wasn't impressed. "That's not a lot!"

"No, it's not," I allowed, "but considering that it costs me only $10 a month to run my Web site, it was already covering my expenses. It also encouraged me to add more content to my site in order to attract more visitors. After a few months, I was making between $20 and $60 a month. Again, I wasn't getting rich, but I was making money. I think it's a realistic range for a lot of sites."

"But then," I continued, "I got lucky." And I told Claude my Vioxx story.

The Vioxx Recall

In September of 2004, the pharmaceutical giant Merck & Co., Inc., announced that it was voluntarily withdrawing Vioxx, one of its star drugs, from the market. (Note that Vioxx is a registered trademark of Merck & Co., Inc.) They did this because of a study that showed that long-term users of Vioxx, a pain reliever popular with arthritis sufferers, had an increased risk of strokes and heart attacks. The recall generated a media frenzy—it was front-page news on most major newspapers the next day.

As it happens, I had been using Vioxx myself at that time for pain relief, but I wasn't a long-term user. So although I wasn't in danger— the risks were only apparent after at least 18 months of use—the recall still gave me pause.

The day after the recall, I had a funny thought. I had actually heard about Vioxx well before my doctor prescribed it. Why? Because

Vioxx

Merck's official Vioxx withdrawal announcement is at www.memwg.com/ vioxx-withdrawal/.

Spam, Spam, Spam

Try www.memwg.com/about-spam for a good overview of what spam is and what you can do about it.

The Vioxx Parody

The full text of my Vioxx parody is available online from the book's Web site at www.memwg.com/vioxx.

Vioxx was prominently featured in many of the unsolicited emails — popularly known as *spam* — that I receive. Wouldn't it be funny if there were a noticeable drop in spam worldwide as spammers scrambled to find an alternative drug to promote?

A Parody Is Born

What started out as a funny thought quickly became a full-fledged humor piece. A couple of hours later, I had transformed the initial joke into a fake press release and placed it on my Web site. Here's how it starts:

> *Pharmaceutical giant Merck's surprise withdrawal yesterday of its anti-arthritis drug Vioxx (also known as rofecoxib) caught more than just Wall Street by surprise. Although most media attention was focused on arthritis sufferers and other patients who were taking Vioxx for general pain relief, spammers — who prefer to call themselves "bulk email providers" — were dealing with their own anxiety issues.*

> *"Vioxx is an important drug for us," says acknowledged spam king Pone Leray. "There are literally millions of people out there with arthritis and similar conditions who have been able to find relief using Vioxx. Now we can't market it to them anymore. We've had to temporarily suspend many of our mailings while we figure out how to best deal with the problem."*

After the parody was up on my site, I sent a link to it to a few of my friends and turned my attention to other things. As I explained to Claude, that's when the excitement really started.

The Ads

I routinely check my AdSense account, even on weekends, because one of the great features about AdSense is that revenue is tracked by the system as it happens, with very little delay. That Saturday — two days after the Vioxx recall and one day after I had written the parody—I made just over $26 from the ads on my site (**Figure 1.4**). This was a much higher value than normal for my site. What had happened?

Saturday, October 2, 2004					Download CSV file
Date ▼	Page impressions	Clicks	Page CTR	Page eCPM [?]	Your earnings
Saturday, October 2, 2004	198	11	5.6%	$134.85	$26.70
Totals	**198**	**11**	**5.6%**	**$134.85**	**$26.70**
Averages	198	11			$26.70

Figure 1.4 First-day earnings from my Vioxx parody.

As it turns out, one of the tongue-in-cheek "predictions" I had made had come true. In the parody, I had a so-called "industry analyst" (whose name is actually an anagram for *what do I know*) talk about the impact of the Vioxx recall on Google's revenues:

> *"Google's revenues might actually increase because now a lot of lawyers and consumer advocacy groups will start buying ads urging people to sue Merck. Lawyers are willing to pay a lot to find the right people to file for class action suits. This could actually be a short-term bonanza for Google."*

This particular prediction was right on the money. Almost overnight, law firms had started placing Vioxx-related advertisements. They smelled opportunity (expensive litigation) and were looking for potential clients. And they were willing to pay to get to them. As I discovered, the lawyers were paying Google several *dollars* per click, an unusually high amount—per-click fees of between 5 and 50 cents are the norm. The Vioxx recall was definitely good for Google, and, by extension, good for me!

The Response

Once I realized what had happened, I knew I had to act quickly in order to capitalize on my good fortune, because interest in Vioxx—and hence the number of available advertisements—would surely wane as time passed. Over the next few days, I worked to make more money from my parody by doing these things:

- Fine-tuning the text of the page.

- Experimenting with the number of ads on the page and their layout.

- Directly telling more people about the page.

- Indirectly telling others about the page by including a link to it as part of my signature in emails and forum postings.

- Adding related pages and linking to them from the original page.

In the end, I made over $350 that month from Vioxx-related content, almost all profit. And it was *fun* to do.

Web Basics

"That's a great story," said Claude after I had finished, "but you got lucky. It doesn't help *me* make money."

"On the contrary," I replied. "Luck played a part, but so did know-how. By fine-tuning and updating the page and directing traffic to the site, I probably doubled my profit."

Claude was still unconvinced. "Sure, but doing all that techie stuff is easy for you. Even if I wrote something good, I still couldn't make a Web page out of it. I'm not a geek, so there's no way that *I* could build a Web site."

"That, my friend, is where you're wrong," I said. It was time to correct his misconceptions about some basic Web terminology.

Web Pages Are Documents

A Web page is just a document. You can even use a word processor to create it, like any other document. You don't believe me? Launch your word processor and look through its menus. Look for a menu or option like "Save as Web page" or "Export as HTML." (*HTML*, short for *hypertext markup language*, is the standard Web page document format.) You're already capable of creating Web pages and you probably didn't know it!

A Web page is a very simple document. That's one of its strengths. In fact, a word processor is usually too complicated a tool to use for creating and editing Web pages. A specialized Web page editor is a much better tool for this purpose, and there are many free ones to choose from (**Figure 1.5**). With a bit of experience, you can even tweak the documents by hand—which sometimes is useful.

HTML for Newbies

Learn the basics of hypertext markup language using the tutorials listed at www.memwg.com/html-tutorials/.

Web Authoring for Free

Find a list of quality Web page authoring freeware at www.memwg.com/html-freeware/.

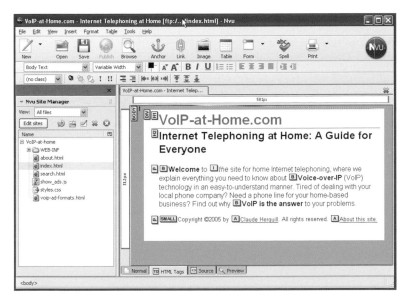

Figure 1.5 Nvu, available at www.nvu.com, is one of many free Web page editors.

From Web Page to Web Site

Once you have a Web *page*, you can build a Web *site*. Let me repeat this point, because I want to emphasize it: *If you can build a Web page, you can build a Web site.* A Web site is just a set of pages that share a common Web address. In other words, the Web site is where the Web page "lives," so to speak, on the Internet.

Although single-page Web sites definitely exist, most sites have multiple pages, often hundreds or thousands of them. But such sites are built one page at a time, so don't feel overwhelmed by the task ahead of you. If you can find time to create one or two pages a week, you'll have 50 to 100 pages on your site in a matter of months. Not that you have to wait that long—you can start making money with your site with just a few pages.

No Programming Required

The kind of Web site you're going to build doesn't require any programming. In technical terms, it's called a *static* site because the Web pages hardly ever change. By contrast, a *dynamic* site has pages that change, either because the content is updated from a database or because the content is generated by small computer programs that vary the material depending on the viewer. Sites like `www.amazon.com` make extensive use of dynamic page generation.

The Web Server Makes It Public

The Web *server* is a software application that exposes a Web site for others to see. You can't have a Web site without a Web server, because the server is what a browser communicates with in order to fetch Web pages. Without the server, your Web site is just a bunch of files sitting in your computer that only you can access.

Unlike a Web site, a Web server is complicated to set up and (especially) to maintain. In fact, there are all kinds of reasons *not* to run the Web server software yourself, even if you're technically inclined. I'll get to that later, but consider this: If *I* don't run a Web server, why should *you*? Let someone else run the Web server for you on their own computer. This is called *Web hosting* and it'll get your site up and running a *lot* faster than setting up your own Web server.

Web Server Confusion

Sometimes *Web server* refers to the physical computer that the Web server software runs on, as opposed to the software itself. To avoid this confusion, I always say *Web server* to refer to the software and *server computer* to refer to the computer on which the Web server runs.

The Web Address

Every public Web site has a Web *address* that distinguishes it from other sites. The address includes a *host name* and a *domain name*. The host name is the name of the computer on which the Web server software runs. The domain name is the public name for a group of computers.

For example, the Web address `www.EricGiguere.com` has the host name `www` (for World Wide Web) and the domain name `EricGiguere.com`. In some cases, the address includes additional information after the domain name, but usually the host name and domain name together are enough to locate a Web site. The host name is important when there are two or more Web servers in a domain, but can normally be dropped otherwise. By convention, the primary Web site in a domain uses the special host name `www`.

History of the Web

An excellent and authoritative history of the Internet and the World Wide Web can be found on the Internet Society's site, www.isoc.org/internet/history/.

Basic Blogging

The blog portal www.blogger.com has a good section on basic blogging. A brief but interesting history of blogging by Dave Winer, author of the longest-running weblog on the Net, is at http://newhome.weblogs.com/historyOfWeblogs.

Your site will need a Web address, so you'll need to obtain a domain name. Finding the right name is harder than it seems. Ideally, the domain name will directly relate to your site's content, because AdSense uses the Web address as one of its inputs when it tries to figure out what your site is really about—so choosing a good name is important.

Blogging for Money

"OK," said Claude, "I think I understand the basics. It does seem pretty simple."

"Absolutely," I told him. "The Web was able to grow quickly because it was built on simple standards. A moderately technical person could download, install, and configure the necessary software in a matter of hours. Web browser software is now bundled with every new computer. Operating systems like Linux and Mac OS X even include built-in Web server software."

"One more thing, then," Claude continued. "Can you tell me the difference between a Web site and a blog? Stef's been telling me that I should 'get with it' and create a blog since I spend so much time on the computer anyhow." Stef is Claude's daughter, who attends a local college.

"When it comes right down to it," I continued, "a blog is just a set of frequently and easily updated pages on a Web site. The term *blog* is short for *weblog*, a type of online diary or journal. For some people, their blog is their entire Web site. For others, a blog is just one component of the Web site. Does Stef have a blog?" Claude indicated that she did. "Then I'd love to talk to her about it. The more advanced features of a blog—letting readers post comments, tracking references by other blogs—require the installation of special software on the Web server, so many bloggers let blogging services like `LiveJournal` or `Blogger`—which, incidentally, is owned by

Google—handle the technical details for them (**Figure 1.6**). These services can host a blog for you on their own Web sites, but most can also publish the blog over to a Web site that you control. I'd be curious to know how she set up her blog."

Claude wasn't sure. "I think she had someone set it up for her. But I know she adds to it herself."

"That's exactly why blogging services are so popular—they make it easy for anyone to create and maintain a blog."

"So should I create a blog or a regular Web site?" he asked me.

Figure 1.6 Google's Blogger weblog service.

"Or maybe both?" I countered. "There's no right answer—it depends if the blog format makes sense for what you want to do or not."

"Can you make money with a blog, too?" I'm not sure if Claude was thinking about himself or his daughter!

"You can display AdSense ads in your blog, yes," I told him. "It's not really any different; you just have to paste the AdSense code into the right spot. I'd be happy to show you or Stef how to do it."

"That would be great," he said. "Let me set something up. I'm sure she'd appreciate your help."

Moving Forward

"You know," Claude continued, "I think Anita would also be interested in learning this stuff." Anita was Claude's eldest daughter. She stayed at home to look after her two young children. "She's always wishing she could do something to make a bit of money while the kids are at school."

"Then she should definitely try making money with Google," I said, "because it doesn't cost anything to join the AdSense program and the costs of setting up a blog or Web site are pretty minimal. Why don't you call her and Stef over to your place sometime? I'll join you and we'll go over how the AdSense program works and you can all decide if you want to try it out or not."

"Perfect!" Claude said. And we agreed to meet in a week or two to talk about AdSense. Which is the topic of the next chapter, of course.

chapter two

Understanding AdSense

> Eric: Tonight I'm going to explain Google's AdSense program to you.

> Anita: Ads annoy me, actually. They're always showing up where I don't want to see them.

> Eric: You're referring to 'pop-up' ads. They are obnoxious. But there are ways to disable them.

> Claude: I see text-only ads all over the place now. Sometimes I even click on them. They're pretty unobtrusive. Google shows them on their search pages, but they don't bother me there.

> Eric: In fact, Google is one of the major players in online advertising. They really pioneered the use of text-only ads. One of the things that makes AdSense so great is that the ads are *context-based*. They're targeted specifically to the content of the Web page on which they appear. That makes them more appealing to the people visiting the page.

The next week I found myself at Claude's house, sitting at the dining room table with him and his grown-up daughters. Claude's wife wasn't interested in our discussion, but she definitely encouraged him to pay close attention—no doubt she was glad that I was keeping him out of her hair.

It was time to get started. "Tonight," I said, "I'm going to explain Google's AdSense program to you. I assume you're all familiar with Web-based advertising?"

"Ads annoy me, actually," said Anita. "They're always showing up where I don't want to see them."

"You're referring to 'pop-up' ads," I said. "They *are* obnoxious. But there are ways to disable them, you know. If you're using Microsoft's Internet Explorer, install the free Google Toolbar and take advantage of its built-in pop-up blocker. Other browsers also have pop-up blockers available."

Stef chimed in. "At my college, they don't even let us run Internet Explorer anymore, because it caused too many problems. Now we all use the free Firefox browser. I haven't seen a pop-up for a while now."

"What about other ads?" I asked. "Do you still see them?"

Claude jumped into the conversation at this point. "Oh sure," he said, "I see them all over the place now, probably more than before. A lot of them are text-only ads, which I don't actually mind so much. Sometimes I even click on them. They're pretty unobtrusive. Google shows them on their search pages, but they don't bother me there—I still get the information I need."

"In fact," I responded, "Google is one of the major players in online advertising. They really pioneered the use of text-only ads. That's why the AdSense program is so appealing. It gives ordinary people like us access to the same pool of ads that Google shows on its own pages. Claude, have you noticed anything special about those ads?"

"You mean the fact that they're related to what I'm searching for?" he asked.

I pointed my index finger right at Claude. "Bingo," I said. "That's what makes AdSense so great. AdSense ads are *context-based* ads. They're targeted specifically to the content of the Web page on which they appear. That makes them more appealing to the people visiting the page. Those visitors are more likely to click the ads, and those who do are likelier to buy something from the advertisers placing the ads. It's a winning scenario for you and your Web pages. More important, it's a winning scenario for advertisers."

"Why does that matter?" Anita asked me.

"Simple," I answered, "advertisers directly or indirectly pay for much of the Web."

Who Pays for the Web?

Stef nodded in agreement, but Claude and Anita seemed surprised by that. "I thought," Claude said, "that the Web was started by the government. You know, for military research."

"You're confusing the Web and the Internet, Claude," I said. "The Internet came first. As you said, its roots were in the military. Originally, the Internet linked educational, research, military, and governmental organizations together for noncommercial purposes. It was considered 'dirty' to use the Internet for purely commercial purposes."

"Not any more!" said Stef.

"No," I agreed, "so things have changed. But the Web we know today began in the early 90s as a simple collaboration tool for physicists and other scientists. The Internet already existed, but it was mostly used for file transfers and email, not interactive browsing."

Stef was surprised. "People traded music even back then?"

Web Origins

Learn more about Tim Berners-Lee and the origins of the Web at www.memwg.com/ history-of-the-web.

TINSTAAFL

Influential economist Alvin Hansen (d. 1975), who helped introduce Keynesian economic theory into American policy-making, was one of the designers of the Social Security system. He is usually cited as the originator of the acronym TINSTAAFL, for "There is no such thing as a free lunch."

"Well, not really," I said, "that came later. But before the Web, there was—and still is—a lot of free software you could download along with all kinds of useful information. The Web made it much easier to do these things, though, and as the Internet grew, so did the Web. Today there are billions of pages on the Web, most of which are available to anyone with a Web browser and an Internet connection."

The Origins of the World Wide Web

Oddly enough, the Web did not originate in a computer science laboratory, but in a European nuclear research facility known at that time as CERN and now called the European Organization for Nuclear Research. A researcher there, Tim Berners-Lee, wrote a proposal called *Hypertext and CERN* that led directly to the creation of what we now refer to as the World Wide Web.

"For free!" Stef said.

"They certainly seem to be," I agreed. "But are they really? Alvin Hansen said it best: There's no such thing as a free lunch. Well, there's no such thing as a free Web, either—*someone* has to pay for it." And then I explained why advertising is so important for the Web.

The Web Is a Communications Medium

The Web is a communications medium, a means of mass communication comparable to television or radio and yet different because it's a two-way, interactive medium. Some people compare the Web to a giant library, but that's a weak analogy: A library centralizes and classifies information, while the Web is decentralized and anarchistic by its very nature.

Even if the information being communicated is free, the medium itself isn't free. It costs money to build and run the Web, just as it costs money to build and run television or radio stations. We pay for these things in different ways. As individuals, we pay for Internet access from our homes. Companies and other organizations also pay to connect their offices to the Internet, but then they also invest money to develop and maintain Web sites and other Internet-based services. Internet service providers pay for much of the infrastructure that ties it all together.

In other words, everyone pays something, directly or indirectly, to keep the Web running. In particular, the costs of running a Web site can vary dramatically based on how many people visit it, especially if they're downloading files from the site. To pay these costs, or even turn a profit, many Web sites turn to advertising.

Advertising and the Web

Conventional print and broadcast media—newspapers, radio, and television being the typical examples—fund themselves in different ways. Some sell subscriptions. Some sell advertising space. Some ask for donations. Many use a mixture of funding models—you probably don't find it unusual to buy a newspaper full of advertisements, or to pay cable fees to watch television programs peppered with commercials.

These funding models also work for content-oriented Web sites—in other words, sites that aren't directly selling products or services. Subscription-based sites offer readers exclusive content that is limited to those who are willing to pay for the privilege of reading it. Many small, independent sites rely on monetary donations to get by. And, of course, advertisements are displayed on many sites. Again, funding models might be combined: It's not unusual for an ad-supported site to have a subscribers-only section, for example, where subscribers have access to additional content or services.

No model is perfect. Subscription-based sites have to convince people to spend money for content and services whose value may not be

Easy Donations

Large Web companies like eBay (through its PayPal Donations program, see www.memwg.com/paypal-donations) and Amazon.com (through its Amazon Honor System program, see www.memwg.com/amazon-honor-system) now make it easy for nonprofit Web sites to receive donations from page visitors.

Ad News

The Clickz site www.clickz.com/news/ provides a daily insider's report on the Internet advertising industry— its trends, events, and personnel.

apparent, especially when competing sites already offer the same things for free. Donation-supported sites depend entirely on the kindness and generosity of their visitors. And advertising-based sites give up valuable screen real estate for use as ad space.

Of the three models, however, advertising is the best bet for a content-oriented site to make money, because you don't need to sell and manage subscriptions (which can be complicated) or ask for (and perhaps never receive) donations. Deliver enough viewers to the advertisers (which isn't always easy) and you'll probably make some money.

The proof? You'll find advertising on all kinds of commercial sites, not just the large ones (**Figure 2.1**). And it's not just media outlets. Advertising is *everywhere* on the Web. Even online retailers like Amazon.com display advertisements: Each book description at Amazon.com includes a section of sponsored links related to the book's subject and/or author. (A *sponsored link* is one that has been placed on the page by an advertiser through a special arrangement— in the case of Amazon.com, the links are supplied by Google, the same company that offers AdSense.)

As you might imagine, though, selling advertising space and then displaying the advertisements can be a lot of work. That's why advertising services like AdSense were created to do most of the work. All you do is decide where to show the ads on your site, and for a cut of the revenue the service does the rest.

Web Advertising 101

At this point, I think all three of them understood how important advertising is to the Web. Stef had actually taken an advertising course at college, so it wasn't news to her. "We spent a couple of classes discussing online advertising," she said, "but it's a pretty broad topic and we didn't have time to cover it all. There were a lot of details, though, a lot of terms to understand and memorize."

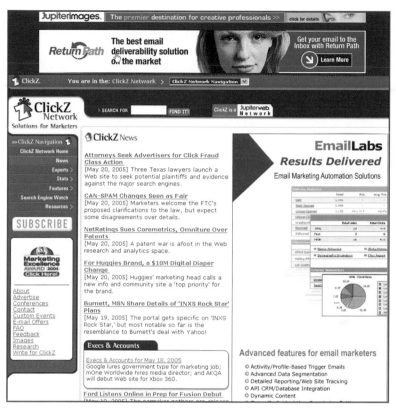

Figure 2.1 The ClickZ Network, an Internet advertising report, is itself powered by extensive advertising in several locations and formats.

"I'm not surprised," I said, "because online advertising *is* a broad topic. But we're looking at a narrower topic, Web-based advertising, and it's important that we all understand basic Web advertising concepts." I then gave them a crash course in Web advertising.

Ad Formats

The *format* of an advertisement refers to its type and its position on a page. The first advertisement format on the Web was the *banner ad*, a clickable rectangular image (wider than it is tall) displayed at

Banner Blindness

Animation and other eye-grabbing techniques are sometimes used to combat banner blindness—see www. memwg.com/banner-blindness for more details.

Block Those Pop-Ups

For more on pop-up ads and how to block them, see www.memwg.com/ pop-up-blockers.

the top of a Web page. In order to accommodate limited screen sizes—remember, this was back when Windows-based screen resolutions of 640 pixels wide by 480 pixels high were still common— banners at the time were fairly small; a popular size was 468 pixels wide by 60 pixels high.

Banner ads are still used today, though they're often larger than the early banners. However, one problem with banner ads is that Web page visitors often ignore them. This phenomenon was first described in 1998 by researchers at Rice University, who called it *banner blindness*.

Other image-based advertisement formats used today include the *tower ad* (basically a vertical banner ad shown to the left or right of content) and the *inline ad* (an ad inserted in the middle of content). Some ads are even interactive, letting the visitors play games or take quizzes. Another format that's becoming popular is the *video-based ad*, such as the series created for American Express featuring comedian Jerry Seinfeld and an animated Superman character.

Image ads are generally inoffensive, though sometimes the animations are annoying. More annoying are the aggressive ad formats that actively interfere with the viewing of a Web page. The most infamous of these is the *pop-up ad*, an ad that literally pops up in a new browser window. This has led to the creation of special pop-up blockers like the ones used by Stef and Claude. (There is also a related and slightly less offensive format called a *pop-under*, in which the new browser window opens underneath the existing window instead of on top of it.) To combat pop-up blockers, advertisers sometimes use alternative formats like *sliding ads* (ads that appear to slide around the Web page, covering some of the content until they are dismissed) and *interstitials* (ads that are shown when a visitor jumps between pages).

Compared to visually-oriented advertisements, text-based advertisements are plain and simple. A *text ad*—also called a *sponsored link*— is a block of descriptive text that links to an advertiser's Web site.

Interested readers will follow the link to learn more about the product or service that the advertiser is promoting. Subtle visual clues like borders, spacing, and shading distinguish text ads from the actual content of the page.

Text ads work well in places where image ads are too constrained (there's not enough space to show the image) or somehow inappropriate (such as on pages that are mostly text and have very simple formatting). Search engines and Web directories like Google and Yahoo! make extensive and effective use of text ads. Also, you don't have to be a graphic designer or use special software to create appealing text ads. You can string a set of text ads together horizontally or vertically to form text ad "banners" or embed the ads directly into the page content (**Figure 2.2**).

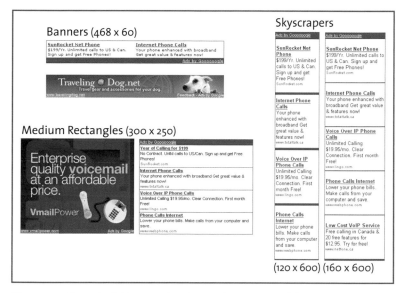

Figure 2.2 Sample AdSense ads. Many other sizes and formats are available. Note that image-based ads are also offered.

Ad Argot

Fastclick offers a specialized and useful glossary of Web advertising jargon at www.fastclick.com/pu_glossary.html.

Ad Costs

Conventional media charge advertisers fees based mostly on the number of people who are going to see or hear an advertisement. In a magazine, for example, a full-page advertisement near the front costs more than a small ad buried in the back because more readers will see the first ad. In television, the cost to air a commercial alongside a hit show is substantially more than the cost for a show that nobody's watching.

These media are really charging based on *impressions*, the number of times a human has seen or heard an advertisement. Calculating impressions is mostly educated guesswork, based primarily on raw circulation or viewer numbers. This is why television and radio stations are so concerned with their ratings in key demographic segments of the population, such as 18-to-35-year-olds: The stations with higher ratings can charge more for commercials and other promotions.

Web sites often charge advertisers by impression. Impression tracking seems easier with a Web site because the Web server knows precisely how many times a given page has been accessed. But it's not that simple, unfortunately. Page data may be *cached* (copied) by a closer Web server known as a *proxy server*, so not all page accesses are tracked by the original Web site. On the other hand, access counts get inflated by *crawlers*, automated Web site analysis and cataloging tools used by Google and other search engines, which fetch pages without displaying them.

Advertisers really want to track how many *humans* are exposed to a given advertisement. Counting page accesses—even accounting for proxy servers and crawlers—is easy, but it isn't very accurate. Some visitors turn off images and don't see image-based ads. Some run ad-blocking software and don't see *any* ads. Even tracking unique Internet addresses isn't enough, because at large companies it's possible for thousands of computers to share a single public Internet address. That's why advertising services often use *cookies* and similar techniques to track individuals. None of these methods is perfect, however.

One alternative to tracking impressions is to track clicks. In other words, instead of charging based on the (estimated) number of people who *view* an ad, charge advertisers based on the number of people who *click* the ad. This is sometimes referred to as *pay-per-click* advertising, since the advertiser only pays when someone clicks on the ad.

Advocates of pay-per-click advertising consider that counting clicks is a more accurate measure of the effectiveness of an advertisement. The counting itself is trivial: The click takes the user to a special Web site run by the advertising service that records the click details—which ad was clicked on which page—and then sends the user to the final destination as determined by the advertiser. The final destination is usually a page on the advertiser's Web site. The advertiser can easily determine which ad the visitor clicked, too, giving the advertiser valuable information about its ad campaign. (Note that the ads shown in impression-based advertising can also be clicked and also provide valuable context data to the advertiser, but the advertiser pays whether the ad is clicked or not.)

Normally, each click in a pay-per-click scheme represents a particular individual interested in learning more about a product or service. The assumption is that an individual will click a given ad only once and that a click demonstrates that the person is interested in the advertiser's offering. In other words, the individual who arrives at the advertiser's site due to a click is a *prequalified sales lead*, a potential customer with an expressed interest in what the advertiser sells. These are valuable people, because they're more likely than the general public to buy the advertiser's products or services. That's what makes pay-per-click advertising so appealing: The advertiser gets a measurable, prequalified stream of visitors to its Web site.

Have a Cookie

A cookie is a small piece of data stored in a Web browser on request by a Web site and returned to the Web site whenever the browser revisits it. See www.memwg.com/cookies for more information.

Which is the better model, impression tracking or click tracking? It really depends on what the advertiser is trying to achieve. For overall brand awareness, maybe impression tracking is better. For individual product sales, click tracking may make more sense. These are the kinds of issues that advertisers have to grapple with in order to make the best use of limited advertising budgets.

Click Fraud

One problem with pay-per-click advertising is that it is more susceptible to fraud than impression-based advertising. Pay-per-click fraud is often referred to as *click fraud*, and there are two common scenarios.

The first scenario occurs when a competitor or a disgruntled customer (or even worse, a *group* of disgruntled customers) clicks a specific advertiser's ads. Each click costs the advertiser some money, depleting its budget for that particular advertising campaign and bringing the campaign to a premature stop. This also means that some of the visitors arriving at the advertiser's site are not interested in buying anything from the company.

The second scenario is more problematic and occurs when an advertising service shares its revenues with third parties. Unscrupulous Web-site owners arrange for others to randomly click ads on their sites in order to generate additional revenue. They may pay people to do this, farming out the work to people in different countries, or they may build automated systems for doing it. Either way, the advertisers lose.

As you can imagine, the advertising services do their best to combat click fraud. Amateurish click fraud is easy to spot—somebody who quickly clicks several links on a site within the span of a few seconds and from the same Web address is obviously not looking at the advertisements. A well-designed scheme is harder to track down, but the services are getting better at it. They have to—if they allow too much click fraud, the advertisers will lose faith in the pay-per-click method and the services will lose their revenue stream. It's definitely a challenge for them. As you can imagine, these companies take click fraud very seriously.

Click Fraud

The chief financial officer of Google, for example, has publicly stated that click fraud threatens Google's business mode. See www.memwg.com/click-fraud for the details.

Don't Be Part of the Problem

Once your Web site is up and running, don't become an unintentional party to click fraud. When you tell friends and family about your site, ask them to avoid clicking the ads just to make you money. They may think they're doing you a favor by clicking ads at random, when in fact they're jeopardizing your membership in the AdSense program. The same thing applies to you: *Don't click ads on your own site!* Let your regular visitors click the ads.

AdSense in a Nutshell

Claude took a lot of notes during my lecture on Web advertising, but his daughters seemed content just to listen. After taking a short break, we resumed our discussion.

"That was a pretty good summary," he said, "and it explained a lot to me that I didn't really understand before. Now that we understand the basics, can we talk about AdSense?"

"Sure," I replied. "AdSense is interesting. Most advertising services are designed for large sites that get a lot of traffic. Typically, there's some human interaction involved, where the advertising service works closely with Web site owners to select the type and placement of ads. Dealing with small sites simply isn't economically feasible in this scenario."

"With AdSense," I continued, "Google created an advertising service that is almost completely automated. This is why Google can offer the service to almost anyone who wants it, including small sites like the one you're going to build."

"So how exactly does it work, then?" Anita asked. "It sounds like there's a lot of complicated programming involved."

I shook my head. "No, not for the Web site owners. For them, it's easy. Google does all the hard work." And I explained to them how AdSense works.

How AdSense Works

When you join the AdSense program, you become an AdSense *publisher*. It's an apt name because it really reflects what you'll be doing: publishing Google-supplied ads on your Web site (or sites — you're not actually restricted to a single site).

The AdSense program is easy to understand. Here's how it works:

▶ After being accepted as an AdSense publisher, you get access to a Google-run Web site—which we'll call the *publisher management console*—that lets you manage your AdSense account (**Figure 2.3**).

▶ Using the management console, you select the ad format and color scheme best suited to your site. It's very easy, and you can preview what the ads will look like without doing anything to your site.

▶ Google then generates some code that you paste directly into your Web pages. This code is written in a programming language called JavaScript, but you don't need to know the details; you just put the code on your Web pages—remember, there's no programming required to use AdSense! Embedded in the code are your *publisher ID* (your AdSense account number) and details about the kind of ads you want displayed on the page.

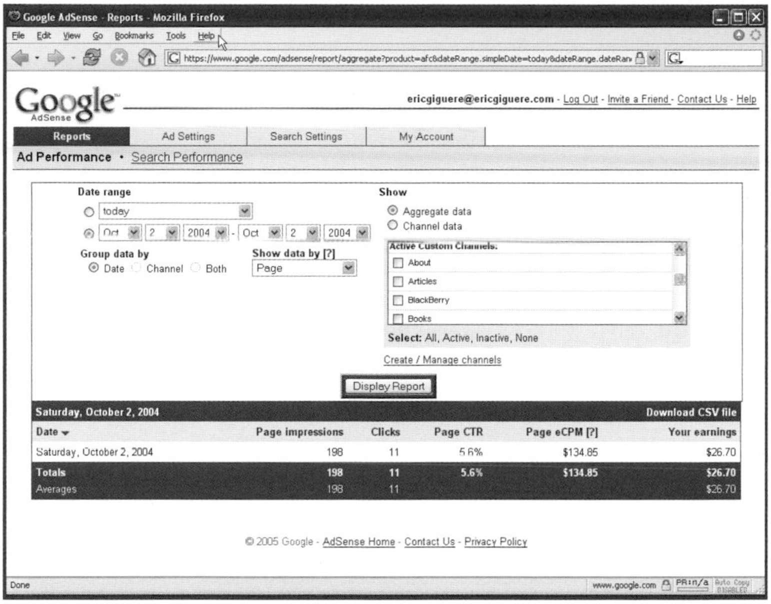

Figure 2.3 The AdSense publisher management console.

▶ Whenever one of your pages is displayed in a browser, the JavaScript code runs. (This assumes the browser has JavaScript enabled—if not, no ads will ever be displayed.)

▶ The first few times the code runs on a particular page, no paying ads are displayed because Google doesn't know what the page is about yet. Public-service advertisements—ads that Google offers free of charge to charitable organizations and that do not make you any money—are displayed on the page in the meantime.

▶ Meanwhile, Google's computers fetch the page in order to analyze it. Normally, the page analysis occurs a few minutes after the JavaScript code runs for the very first time.

▶ Once the page has been analyzed, relevant ads appear when the page is displayed (or refreshed) in the browser. Each ad has a link back to Google. Encoded in these links is information about the publisher (you) and the advertiser.

- ▶ Whenever someone clicks an ad, the visitor's browser is sent to one of Google's Web sites to record the click using the information encoded in the link. Google then quickly redirects the browser to the advertiser's site.

- ▶ For each click, the advertiser is charged a fee, and part of that fee is credited to your account. You can use the management console at any time to see how much money you've made.

Of course, behind this simple process is sophisticated technology and clever programming. Not only must AdSense accurately analyze Web pages and match them to relevant advertisements, it must also detect click fraud and other suspicious activities. And of course, it needs to be up and running every minute of every day. Building an automated advertising service like AdSense is something only a few companies could manage, so you have to give Google credit for building it and letting you reap the benefits of that automation.

AdSense Patents

Google has patents on several aspects of the AdSense program. If you're really curious about AdSense's original design, you can read the patent documents online at the U.S. Patent and Trademark Office's Web site. See www.memwg.com/adsense-patents for the links.

Where the Ads Come From

Anita wondered where the ads come from, which is a perfectly reasonable question to ask. After all, if there aren't many ads available to display, what's the point in using the AdSense program?

Most of the ads available to AdSense publishers are text ads from Google's AdWords program. These are the same ads that are displayed on Google's search-results page, where they're called "Sponsored Links." (Note that advertisers can choose not to have their ads displayed on third-party Web sites, so Google itself actually has a larger ad pool to draw from than the AdSense publishers do.) The ads are clearly separated from the search results, and Google has always said that the ads have no influence on how searches are performed.

An AdWords text ad has four lines of text: a title, a two-line description, and a display URL. Conciseness is important, since the title is limited to 25 characters and the other lines (including the URL) are limited to 35 characters each. The ad also has a destination URL that isn't shown. This is the actual link that sends visitors to the advertiser's Web site.

Each text ad is associated with one or more *keywords*. A keyword is a word or phrase that represents or summarizes a key concept, idea, or attribute of the product or service being advertised. For example, a tire retailer might use keywords like "tire," "snow tire," "radial tire," and even brand names like "Michelin" and "Bridgestone." AdWords will even suggest related keywords to the advertiser, which makes selecting the right keywords even easier.

Keywords are important because an ad only appears on pages related to its keywords. Only a limited number of ads can appear on a given page, so Google uses an auction-based system that lets advertisers bid for the chance to show their ads. The bidding system has a feedback component to it to ensure that the ads with high clickthrough rates— ads that are clicked often—are given priority over other ads, even higher-paying ones. In fact, nonperforming ads are eventually dropped by the AdWords system in order to make room for the ones that get good response. Advertisers also set a daily *budget* to limit their advertising costs—ads are not shown for the rest of the day once the budget's been exceeded.

AdWords

For a detailed tutorial of the AdWords program, go to www.google.com/ads/.

The AdWords program also supports image ads, but only for display on third-party Web sites. The keyword bidding system used for text ads is also used for image ads.

There are more text ads than image ads available through AdWords, mostly because Google does not display image ads on its own pages. Neither are AdSense publishers forced to display them—by default, publishers get only text ads. A publisher can ask (through the AdSense management console) to receive both text and image ads, or image ads only.

How Ads Are Selected

"So how does Google know which ads to display on a page?" Claude asked me. "It doesn't sound simple." And Claude was right: It's not simple. But neither is it as hard as you might think.

AdSense matches ads to Web pages (also called *content pages*) using special algorithms developed by Google. Keywords are at the heart of those algorithms, as you've probably guessed by now, since the AdWords program—the source of the ads—is itself keyword-based. Once a page's keywords have been determined, relevant ads are easily selected from the AdWords ad pool. So the real trick is figuring out the keywords for a given page.

Since AdSense is an automated system, the algorithms must determine an accurate set of keywords for a content page without requiring human involvement. Many of the details are actually revealed in the original AdSense patent application that Google filed with the U.S. Patent and Trademark Office. Here are some of the criteria used by the AdSense algorithms:

> ▶ The frequency with which a keyword appears within a Web page. The more times a keyword appears on the page, the more relevant it is to the page content.

- The infrequency with which a keyword appears across a set of Web pages. The more common the keyword, the less relevant it is to the page content.

- The results of analyzing other pages in a set of Web pages, including pages that link to or are linked from the page. The keywords of previously analyzed pages may be relevant to the current page.

- The title of a page. Keywords in the title are assumed to be more relevant.

- The text in the links from other pages to the page. Again, keywords in such text are assumed to be more relevant.

This list is by no means exhaustive, but it shows you the kind of analysis that AdSense does in order to place relevant advertisements on a Web page. The algorithms aren't always right, but Google adjusts them from time to time in order to achieve better accuracy.

AdSense Highlights

Stef was impressed by what she heard. "My friend John, the guy who set up my blog for me, is always raving about Google and the cool things they do. I guess this is one of them!"

"They've definitely created a cool system," I agreed. "What's really interesting about AdSense, though, is how quickly it's evolved. The AdSense program was actually fairly limited when it was introduced in 2003: There were only four ad sizes to choose from, image ads were not supported, and there was no detailed tracking of visitor clicks. Publishers asked for more features, however, and soon these limitations were removed." I then summarized the important features.

Nix the Pix

Web pages that are primarily graphics and multimedia, not text—as on a site for an art studio—are difficult for AdSense to analyze and may not return relevant ads. Important keywords should always be included as text on your pages.

Different Ad Types

AdSense offers two types of ads: conventional text and image ads, which jump directly to an advertiser when clicked, and *ad links*, which open a page of ads when clicked. Ad links list topics, not individual advertisements. Ad links are more compact than the traditional type of advertisement, but when they are clicked they display more ads than you'd see normally.

Multiple Ad Formats and Sizes

AdSense supports three regular ad formats, with several ad sizes in each format. A particular combination of an ad format and an ad size is referred to as an *ad unit*. Each ad unit displays a set of text ads or a single image ad. (Ad links all follow the same general format, though their size and the number of links varies. The units are referred to as *ad links units*.)

The first format is the *banner* format, the classic rectangular advertisement format where the width is substantially larger than the height. Each text ad in a banner is the same height as the banner itself (**Figure 2.4**). A wide banner is sometimes called a *leaderboard*.

Figure 2.4 A sample AdSense banner ad.

The second format is a *tower* (**Figure 2.5**). A tower is basically the opposite of a banner, its height substantially larger than its width. Text ads are as wide as the banner and are stacked on top of each other. A tower is also called a *skyscraper*.

The final format is the *inline rectangle*, a rectangle whose dimensions are roughly (or even exactly) equal. Unlike banners and towers, which are normally placed on the edges of a Web page, inline rectangles are often inserted directly in the middle of a Web page (**Figure 2.6**). Text ads shown with the inline rectangle format are stacked on top of each other just as they are in the tower format.

A good selection of sizes is available within each format. The smallest sizes display one or two text ads, while the largest display four or five. Note that image ads are supported by only a few of the sizes, so your choices are more limited if you want to display image ads within an ad unit.

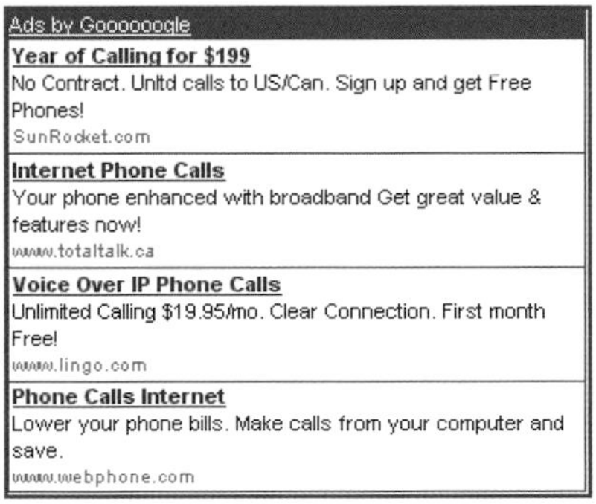

Figure 2.6 A sample inline rectangle ad.

Figure 2.5
A sample tower ad.

Flexible Ad Unit Placement

You can place AdSense ads anywhere on a page as long as visitors don't confuse them with the actual content of the page. Google helps avoid any confusion by drawing a border around the ad unit and by labeling the ad unit with "Ads by Google" or words to that effect, though you can remove the border by changing its color.

Up to three ad units can be placed on a single page. Many sites display just one ad unit per page—you don't want to overwhelm visitors with advertisements. Each ad unit can be a different size and

Add Ad Units

Start with just one ad unit and see if that fills up. If it does, then add more units.

format, though, so it's not uncommon to see pages with a tower on the side and an inline rectangle right in the middle of the page text.

A downside to using multiple ad units on a page is that there may not be enough ads available to fill them all and you may end up with wasted space on the page.

Customizable Color Palettes

The default AdSense color scheme is the same scheme used for sponsored links on Google's own search pages: blue title, black text, green URL, white background. Not every site looks like Google's site, though, so AdSense lets you change the colors to suit your own site's color scheme. Even different ad units on the same page can have different color schemes.

An individual color scheme is referred to as a *color palette*. AdSense includes a number of predefined palettes that can be used by many sites. These palettes have colorful names like "Mother Earth" and "Peach Melba." If none of the built-in palettes suits your needs, though, you can create your own custom palettes.

For variety, each ad unit can rotate through as many as four different color palettes, though a single palette per unit is the norm.

Alternative Advertisements

Despite its best efforts, AdSense can't always fill an ad unit with relevant advertisements. This can occur for a variety of reasons:

- ▶ No or few ads match your content.

- ▶ The only ads available are ones that you're currently blocking (see the section on ad filtering below).

- ▶ There are matching ads, but the advertisers have exceeded their daily budgets.

As long as one or more ads are available, AdSense displays them and fills the rest of the ad unit with the background color. The problem occurs when there are *no* ads to display. Rather than show an empty box, AdSense displays one or more public-service advertisements— *PSAs* for short—in the ad unit. PSAs are free advertising that Google offers to charitable and other nonprofit organizations. Visitors can click PSAs in the same way as they click normal ads, but you don't make any money from those clicks. If you want to make money, you want to avoid PSAs.

Instead of displaying PSAs, you can ask Google to display alternative content in the ad space by providing Google with the URL of some other Web content. The URL might point to an image you've placed elsewhere on your site, to a page fragment you've created, or even to a different advertising service. It doesn't matter what it is, as long as it fills the space allocated for the ad unit. (The space will not be boxed or labeled by Google, of course.)

If you don't have any alternative content to display, you can simply display a colored box that matches the color of the surrounding page area, effectively erasing the ad unit from the page.

Channel Tracking

When AdSense was first introduced, there was no way to track which pages on a Web site were generating the most revenue. After receiving many complaints about this, Google allowed publishers to group pages into *channels* and track revenue on a per-channel basis. Publishers could create up to 50 (the limit's since been increase—see Chapter 7) custom channels to spread however they wanted across their sites.

One problem with custom channels is that they require modification of the AdSense JavaScript code that gets pasted into each Web page. AdSense will generate the modified code for you, but you have to generate the code for each channel and paste it into the appropriate

Black Hole Ads

If you're truly adventurous, you can even make empty ad units collapse to nothing—see www .memwg.com/collapsing -ads for the details.

pages. For a large site, this becomes a bit of a maintenance headache, especially if the AdSense code is otherwise identical across all pages. AdSense now lets you create *URL channels*, channels that track revenue based solely on Web addresses. You can create channels for each page, for groups of pages, or for entire Web sites, all using the exact same AdSense code.

URL-Based Ad Filtering

Sometimes you don't want to see certain ads appearing on your site, especially if those ads are promoting products or services that directly compete with the ones that your site is promoting. AdSense lets you indirectly block these ads using a facility called *URL filtering*.

URL filtering blocks ads based on the Web addresses they link to. You provide AdSense with a list of Web addresses—up to 200 of them—and AdSense ensures that no ads that link to those addresses appear on your pages. It's not a perfect solution by any means, but it works well enough for most sites.

Detailed Reporting

From the publisher's standpoint, one of the great features of AdSense is the detailed reporting available through the AdSense management console. You can track revenue by date and channel and even know when Google has mailed you a payment check. And the great thing is that the really important information—*how much money have I made today?*—is updated continually throughout the day as visitors click the ads on your site.

Monthly Payment

Another great thing about AdSense is that Google pays publishers on a monthly basis. About 20 to 30 days after the end of a month,

Google mails each publisher a check for the prior month's earnings. Note that you'll only receive a check if you've earned at least $100; otherwise, your earnings will be rolled over into the next month.

AdSense for Search

There was one more AdSense feature I needed to discuss. "Everything we've discussed so far about AdSense has been about placing ads on third-party Web pages," I said. "Google refers to this as *AdSense for content*, because it's all about Web-page content. This is the main AdSense program, the one that everyone uses." The three of them nodded their understanding.

"There is a second AdSense program available," I continued, "called *AdSense for search* that appeals to a more limited audience."

"Is it for other search engines?" Anita asked.

"No," I answered. "In fact, one of the conditions of joining the AdSense program—we'll get to those shortly—is that you don't display ads on any search-result pages you might have on your site. In other words, you can't compete with Google's bread and butter, however minuscule that competition might be, and use Google to make money at it."

"I guess that makes sense," Anita said. "So what is AdSense for search, then?"

"AdSense for search is about getting your visitors to use Google for their searching," I explained. "If you direct your visitors to Google's search engine, Google is willing to share some of the advertising revenue with you. Joining AdSense for search gives you the right to display a Google search box on your site. Visitors who enter queries into that search box are sent to a custom Google search page. The search page displays your logo and displays search results generated using the Google search engine. Search-related advertisements are

AdSense for Content

The introductory AdSense for Content page is at www.google.com/adsense/afc-online-overview.

AdSense for Search

Learn more about AdSense for Search at www.google.com/adsense/ws-overview.

displayed prominently at the top of the page. Just as with AdSense for content, you make money if visitors click those ads."

Claude wasn't sure what the benefit of this program was: "Why wouldn't the visitors just go to www.google.com or use their browser's search box? I normally use the Google Toolbar for my searching."

"Because it's a simple way for visitors to search your site," I explained, "not just the Web. It's not a great money-maker for most sites, but if you want to add searching capabilities to your site without having to do any programming, it's an easy way to do it. We'll talk a bit about it later, but really most of our focus is on AdSense for content. I'm just mentioning it because it's an interesting and underused feature."

Joining AdSense

"All right," Claude said, "you've sold me. How do I join AdSense? Do I have to sign away the rights to my firstborn?" Anita rolled her eyes, clearly unimpressed.

I continued my description of AdSense. "Joining AdSense is a simple process—you apply online and wait for Google's approval."

"Does it cost anything?" Stef asked.

"No, there are no fees," I answered, "and once you're approved you can start earning money almost immediately. There are a few conditions, though."

The Application Process

The AdSense program is open to most Web-site owners who meet Google's standards for content and service. You apply online from Google's AdSense site at www.google.com/adsense. The first part of the application process involves creating an AdSense account using your email address and a password you choose. If you already have an account with one of Google's other services (such as AdWords or Google Print, but not GMail), you can reuse your existing login. You then choose the type of account you want to create (individual or business—see below) and provide Google with the important details, such as your name and address.

As part of the application process, you *must* supply the address of a working Web site that you own and control. After you submit the application, someone at Google visits your site to ensure that it meets the AdSense program requirements. This visit normally occurs within two or three days of the application. Google notifies you by email if your application is accepted or refused.

Read the Fine Print
Acceptance into the AdSense program is also conditional on your reading and agreeing to the Terms and Conditions found at www.google.com/adsense/terms.

What If You're Refused?

If your AdSense application is refused, it usually means there's a problem with your Web site. If the reason isn't obvious, you can always contact AdSense support at adsense-support@google.com and ask for clarification. Normally, sites are rejected because they don't meet the AdSense program policies. If you can change your site so that it meets those policies, you can reapply to join AdSense.

This surprised Claude. "So you can't join without a site?"

"Nope," I said.

"So I asked you a useless question," he said.

"No again," I replied, "because you want to keep the content restrictions and other AdSense program policies firmly in mind when you design and build your site. Knowing these things at the start will save you a lot of work later."

AdSense Policies

Read AdSense's program policies at www.google.com/adsense/policies.

"And I have to reapply for each site I create?" he asked.

"Luckily, you don't," I said. "You only have to submit *one* site to Google for approval. Once you've been accepted into the AdSense program, you can display AdSense ads on any site you own that doesn't violate the AdSense program policies. The corollary to this is that you can only have *one* AdSense account. Which isn't that big a deal, since you can easily track which pages on which sites are making you money."

Now it was time to describe the biggest condition on AdSense membership—the AdSense content restrictions.

Content Restrictions

As a mainstream advertising service, AdSense must ensure that participating sites are acceptable advertising venues for the majority of Google's advertising clients. In addition, different legal restrictions in different countries—don't forget that Google's services are available across the world—also limit the kinds of sites that Google wants to associate with. The AdSense program policies therefore place the following restrictions on participating sites:

▶ No pornography or other adult-oriented material.

▶ No discriminatory, hate-inducing, or violent content.

▶ No other content that is illegal or that infringes on other people's rights.

▶ A site must not deceive or induce visitors into clicking ads.

▶ A site must not promote or sell prescription drugs, firearms, alcohol, tobacco, or any related products or services.

▶ A site must not annoy or otherwise interfere with visitors' use and enjoyment of the site and other sites.

Your site must also not interfere with Google's analysis of its content in any way, nor fraudulently manipulate its rankings within the Google search engine.

Some of the restrictions are vague. The program policies are fairly explicit in some areas, though. For example, you can refer to AdSense ads on your site only as "sponsored links" or "advertisements."

Adsense Support

If you're ever unsure about AdSense restrictions or other policy questions, you can always email adsense-support@google.com and ask for clarification.

Keeping Tabs on Sites

The AdSense support team at Google regularly checks participating sites to ensure that they are following the AdSense program policies, especially sites that are unusually active. Any violation of those policies can lead to the suspension or cancellation of an AdSense account.

Quality Standards

Besides content restrictions, AdSense also imposes certain technical quality restrictions on participating sites. Again, this is to ensure that sites associated with Google's services (AdSense and AdWords being two of the more prominent services they offer) do not tarnish Google's own reputation for quality and service. The restrictions are fairly basic:

▶ A site must be launched and working, with no "under construction" pages and no broken links.

▶ Visitors must be able to easily navigate the site.

▶ A site must have a proper Web address and be publicly accessible.

▶ A site must be responsive, so that pages load quickly.

You'd want your site to meet these criteria in any case.

Quality Counts

Additional quality guidelines that every site should adhere to can be found at www.google.com/webmaster/guidelines.html.

Adsense and Taxes

A tax information wizard available through the AdSense management console will guide you in selecting the correct tax form to fill out for your AdSense account.

Account Types

There was one last wrinkle to discuss: the AdSense account types. There are two types of accounts, differing primarily by who gets paid. In an *individual* account, the payee is a person, while in a *business* account the payee is a business. Unless you're already running a small business, you'll probably want to sign up for an individual account and have the AdSense payment checks made out directly to your own name. You can then deposit the checks in your own personal bank account.

As a condition of membership, individuals and businesses based in the United States must provide Google with a federal tax identification number before they can receive any payments. Individuals must supply their Social Security number (SSN), while businesses provide their Employer Identification Number (EIN). (If your business is a sole proprietorship and you don't have an EIN, sign up for an individual account.)

The AdSense program is open to individuals and businesses outside the United States, but there is additional paperwork to fill out once you've been accepted into the program. You'll be required to submit one of several different Internal Revenue Service forms in order to receive payment and possibly pay U.S. taxes on the revenue. Google may even be required to withhold a percentage of each payment on behalf of the U.S. government.

Consult a Professional

In general, any payment you or your business receives from AdSense is going to be treated as income and is likely taxable, but the rules, of course, vary from locale to locale. Be sure to consult a qualified tax professional for advice on how to properly handle AdSense payments.

The Next Challenge

We were all feeling pretty tired at this point, and it was late, so it was time to wrap up our session.

"I hope you understand the AdSense program now," I said to the other three.

Anita was tired, but enthusiastic. "It does sound pretty simple," she agreed. "If I had a Web site, I'd be going online right now to join the program!"

"Yeah, that's the problem," Claude said, "you need a site. That's where it gets complicated, I guess."

"No," I disagreed, "building a site isn't that complicated once you get started. We'll get to that later. But first we need to talk about topic selection, how to figure out what your site should be about."

"To maximize the money you'll make?" Anita asked.

"Not just that," I said, "but that's certainly an obvious reason. We'll save it for a separate session, though." I turned to Stef. "You probably don't need to come to the next one because you already have a blog running."

"Yeah," she agreed, "but I don't like the way it looks. I wish I had more control over it."

"We'll get to that, too," I reassured her, "but first I'll need a session with your dad and your sister to talk about possible topics." I turned to the other two. "That is, if you're interested in proceeding?"

"Absolutely," said Claude.

"You bet!" said Anita.

It would take a while for the three of them to digest what they'd just heard, so we set the next meeting time and parted company.

Starting

Content

Design

AdSense

Traffic

chapter three

Finding Something to Say

> **Eric:** Today, we're going to decide what your sites are going to be about.

> **Anita:** Aren't we doing this backwards? Shouldn't we learn how to build a Web site first and then decide what our topic should be?

> **Eric:** You *could* do it that way, but having a firm idea of what the site's going to be about makes the concepts easier to grasp. Besides, I'm sure you'd rather know sooner than later how much money you can make from a given topic.

I met Claude and Anita a few days later at a coffee shop near my house. I brought along my notebook computer to show them a few things via the coffee shop's wireless hotspot. After we ordered our coffees, I got right down to business.

"Today," I started, "we're going to decide what your sites are going to be about."

"I have a question," Anita said. "Aren't we doing this backwards? Shouldn't we learn how to build a Web site first and *then* decide what our topic should be?"

Her question wasn't unexpected, and I had an answer ready. "You *could* do it that way," I agreed, "but I find that having a firm idea of what the site's going to be about makes the concepts easier to grasp. It also gets your subconscious thinking about the topic as early as possible, which will help when you sit down to write some content." Then I grinned. "Besides, I'm sure you'd rather know sooner than later how much money you can make from a given topic."

"You can do that?" asked Claude.

"Only approximately, of course," I said, "by determining relative keyword values. I'll show you how to do this shortly—that's why I brought my laptop. But the topic choice also influences important decisions, like what to name your site."

"And you want to choose a topic that Google won't frown on," Anita added.

I nodded in agreement. "Precisely—you definitely want to avoid topics that violate the AdSense program policies. But, you know, finding something to say isn't just about deciding on a topic: It's about creating compelling, AdSense-friendly content; it's about copyrights; it's about organizing and editing your material."

"Sounds like a lot of work," Claude grunted.

"It *is* work," I said, "but have you noticed that people do it all the time, most for no compensation? What motivates them?"

Why Publish on the Web?

We all sipped our coffees while the two of them considered my question. Anita was the first to answer. "They want to help others?" she asked.

"Good answer!" I said, smiling. "The Internet connects computers together, but the Web connects *people* together. Remember, the Web started as a way for researchers to help one another by sharing information. Individuals have always played an important part in making the Web what it is today.

"Think of all the Web sites built by individuals or small groups," I continued. "There are many examples: Fans build sites devoted to favorite musicians or celebrities; proud parents post family pictures; the sick create support communities for their illnesses and conditions. Most of these sites aren't money-making ventures, but their creators devote substantial time to their upkeep."

"And don't forget blogs," said Anita.

"Blogs are a great example of how individuals affect the Web," I agreed, "because they're so tied to a person or a small group of people. But all a blog does is make it *easy* to publish on the Web. We still need an answer to *why* people create sites and blogs."

"So why do they do it?" Claude asked me.

"In my opinion," I began, "there are four general motivators for individuals to build a Web presence. I refer to these as the *Four F's*: fame, fortune, philanthropy, and fun. They're not exclusive of one another, but one is usually more dominant." And with that, I launched into explanations of each of the Four F's.

Privacy Info

Read about internet privacy issues at www.privacy.org and www.privacyrights.org.

Fame

Fame has always motivated a certain segment of the population. In this context, fame means being well known and respected within a certain group. Stef has achieved a small degree of fame by creating a blog about herself that anyone could read. From what Claude and Anita told me, her blog was a popular read among her college peers. I was sure that Stef was pleased to know she was making an impact with her writings.

Stef's far from unique in her desire to influence others and gain their respect. Within any given community, there are always people who are more knowledgeable or more skilled than others. Many of these take great pleasure in being asked for their opinions and advice. What's different with the Web and the Internet is that these communities can be spread all across the world. Before, celebrity was usually confined to a small geographic area, with only a small group of people—actors, politicians, musicians—able to achieve celebrity on a larger scale.

Fame can also bring danger, though, as many celebrities have discovered, to their dismay. Anita worries that Stef's blog might make her a target for stalkers. There are measures Stef can take to protect her privacy, but the downside of celebrity is that public exposure can make privacy much harder to achieve.

Fortune

Fortune is the classic motivator. Claude wants to make money and he makes no bones about it. The money is what's motivating him to create a Web presence.

Money is an extremely strong motivator. It was the driving force behind the explosive growth of the Internet in the late 1990s. Even today, the Internet is seen as the likeliest way to gain significant wealth in a short time. If you dream of being rich, the Internet is very seductive.

It's important to realize that there's a difference between making money and becoming wealthy, though. Claude's goals are modest and realistic, as yours should be.

Philanthropy

Philanthropy is a motivator that shows up in the most unexpected places, from the most unexpected people. Take Anita as an example. As a busy young mother in a household where money is tight, you'd think money would be her prime motivator. But it's not—she wants to do something that helps others. She just can't afford to spend a lot of money doing it, which is why the AdSense program appeals to her.

The Web's always been a place for individuals to rally others around a cause and to promote the greater good. For some, that cause is the Web itself and the possibilities it provides for free speech and individual expression. For others, the Web is merely another tool in the arsenal of public service, a way to reach more people in more places.

Nonprofits and AdSense for Search

AdSense for search is one program that a nonprofit organization might find beneficial. Instead of displaying advertisements on its Web site, which may be inappropriate, an organization can use AdSense for search and create a custom Web search page. Instead of going directly to the main Google search page, members and friends of the organization can search the Web from the custom search page and benefit the organization when they click sponsored links. Again, precautions have to be taken by the organization to discourage wholesale clicking of advertisements, no matter how well intentioned, because Google will still consider it to be click fraud.

Internet Bubble

An interesting personal take on the Internet Bubble of the late 1990s can be found at www. paulgraham.com/ bubble.html.

Give It Away

Search for philanthropic web sites at www.directory.google. com/Top/Society/ Philanthropy/.

Although I focus on individuals in this book, the techniques described here can be used by groups and organizations of all kinds. All it takes is one or two persons willing to put in the effort on behalf of the group. Even a nonprofit organization can benefit from having a Web site.

Fun

Fun is the final, and perhaps ultimate, motivator. It can be just as strong as the other three. There are people who build Web sites and blogs because they just enjoy doing it. It might be a learning experience for them. It might be a way to communicate with others who have like interests. It's a fun way to spend some time and develop some skills, no different than any other hobby.

Understanding Your Motivations

Which of the Four F's motivates you the most? The primary motivation is definitely going to influence what to expect from your site or blog. If you're interested in making money, for example, you'll want to choose a topic whose keywords have high pay-per-click fees—but be prepared to face some stiff competition from other sites chasing those same rewards. If fame is what drives you, realize that it won't happen overnight and that it requires a much higher level of interaction on your part—blogs are well suited for this. If philanthropy calls to you, you may find the ad pool for your topic to be very small. If you're doing it primarily for fun, though, any money you make will just add to the enjoyment.

Understanding your motivations lets you set realistic expectations for the amount of money you'll make from your site. If the ads on your site generate only a few cents per click and you have few visitors, you won't be making much money. You might not recoup your Web hosting costs. But you may not care: The fact that you're earning *some* money and that there's always the *potential* to earn more may be good enough, especially from a tax viewpoint if you're able to deduct business expenses from your overall income. (As always, contact a qualified tax professional for advice on these matters.)

No matter what your motivations are, though, it really helps to be *interested* in your site's topic. Ideally, it's a topic that's already familiar to you, but don't worry if it's not—being interested in the topic and willing to learn about it will get you just as far (though not as quickly). But you want the topic to be interesting because it will make *updating* the site more appealing. Your work's not over when the site's unveiled. You have to keep updating it, because a fresh, current site attracts more visitors.

Finding the Right Topic

Claude objected to my characterizations. "You make it sound like I'm only in it for the money," he said, "and that Stef just wants to be famous. And she's not even here to defend herself! Anita's the only one who looks good."

"Don't be offended," I said, "because I'm not here to judge you. Money's a motivator for all three of you, otherwise you wouldn't be talking to me about making money with Google. But it's not always the *primary* motivator, and I think it's important to understand that so you can choose the right topic and have realistic expectations."

"I think I know what my topic is already," said Anita. "It's something that really concerns me: obesity in children and young adults. It's a problem due mostly to poor eating habits and a lack of exercise. I've been clipping out newspaper and magazine articles about it for a while now and talking to other mothers about it. It would be nice to share it with others, too."

"That's a great idea, Anita," I said. "What about you, Claude? Any ideas?"

Web and Taxes

Research issues relating to small business deductions at www.irs.gov, www.hrblock.com, or www.selfemployedweb. com/. Note that potential tax deductions may apply to federal, state, and local taxes.

General Research

Good sites for general knowledge and research include Wikipedia (a free, user-written encyclopedia; see www.memwg.com/wikipedia) and Project Gutenberg (free electronic books; see www.memwg.com/project-gutenberg).

He nodded. "Something to do with technology, I think. Maybe making phone calls with your Internet connection?"

"You mean 'voice-over-IP' technology?" I asked.

"Yeah," Claude said. "I've been using it myself at home as a second phone line and it works quite well."

"Sounds pretty good," I said, and then looked at both of them. "So how do you know if the topics you've chosen are any good? What if several different topics appeal—which topic should you choose? Or what if neither of you had a topic in mind—how do you find one?"

"I'm not sure," Claude answered, "but I bet you're going to show us."

"You're right," I said, smiling. "There are no hard-and-fast rules, but I can give you some tips and show you a few things you can do with your computer to find the topic that's right for you."

Fill a Need

An obvious way to find a topic is to fill a need. Have you ever searched the Web for something and not found it? The Web is an incredible repository of information, but there are still many gaps in what's available, so there's always room for more content.

Anytime you find yourself thinking "I wish there was a good site about such-and-such," you've found a potential topic. This is how Claude and Anita basically came up with their topics. For more ideas, ask friends and acquaintances about the kinds of things they've been unable to find. And if you participate in online forums or groups, keep an eye out for questions from other members. Any topic that fills a need is a possible subject for your site.

Mine the Search Engines

Another source of ideas is search-term lists generated by various search engines. Google, for example, publishes weekly lists of the top ten gaining and declining queries it sees, as well as monthly and yearly summaries of search activities. It refers to these lists as the Google *Zeitgeist*, a German term meaning "the spirit of an era" (see www.memwg.com/zeitgeist).

Some search engines also let you see what other people are searching for right now. The SearchSpy service from Dogpile (`www.memwg.com/searchspy`) or Metaspy from MetaCrawler (`www.memwg.com/metaspy`) are tools you can use as additional idea sources.

More Search-Term Lists

Other search engines maintain their own lists of search terms, such as the Yahoo! Buzz Index (www.memwg.com/yahoo-buzz-index) and the Lycos 50 (www.memwg.com/lycos-50).

Check Keyword Values

Can't choose between two topics? Wondering if the topic you've chosen is interesting to advertisers? Pretend you're an advertiser and see what you'd be paying to link your ads to specific keywords. (Claude was so interested in this technique that he kept crowding out Anita by leaning too closely to my laptop.)

Start by making a short list of keywords for each topic. Then visit different advertising services to figure out how valuable the keywords are to the advertisers using those services. How this is done depends on the advertising service. Services worth exploring are Yahoo! Search Marketing (formerly known as Overture) and Google AdWords.

Yahoo! Search Marketing

Yahoo! Search Marketing directly competes with Google in the pay-per-click advertising arena. One of the services it offers to advertisers is its View Bids tool. This tool is available to anyone who visits the Yahoo! Search MarketingAdvertiser Center, not just Yahoo! customers. (Note that the tools in the Advertiser Center may still refer to Overture, not Yahoo! Search Marketing, but they're the same thing.)

The View Bids tool (`www.memwg.com/view-bids-tool`) lets you enter keywords and see how much current Yahoo! advertisers are bidding

Yahoo! Search Marketing Ads

Visit Yahoo!'s Advertiser Center at searchmarketing.yahoo.com/rc/srch/.

for those terms (**Figure 3.1**). The tool is very simple to use: just enter the keyword and the security code. (The security code is embedded in an image that you can easily decode but that most software cannot.) The results of a typical keyword query are shown in **Figure 3.2**. At Claude's request, I used the keyword *voip* for my query, because it's the standard acronym for "voice-over-IP technology."

Although Claude was quite excited by the tool's results, I had to caution him about two things. First, the View Bids tool shows you the *maximum* amount that advertisers are paying for ads. Like AdWords, Yahoo! Search Marketing uses an auction-based ad selection model referred to as "bid for placement." Advertisers may pay less than the maximum amount shown, sometimes much less.

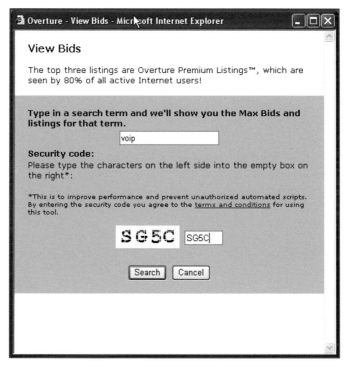

Figure 3.1 Yahoo!'s Search Marketing has a simple keyword bidding tool available to anyone who visits the site.

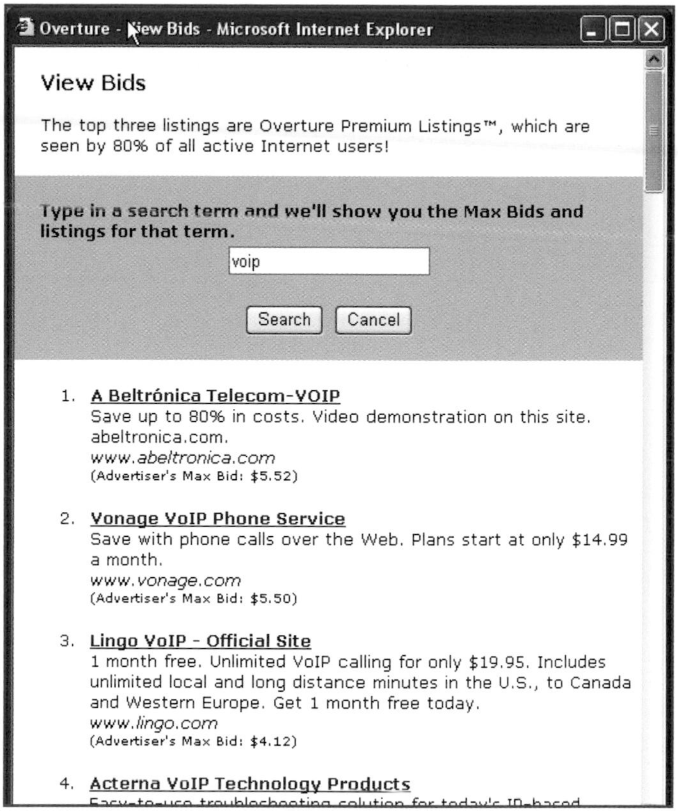

Figure 3.2 A typical keyword search result on Yahoo! Search Marketing.

Bid-for-Placement Patent

Yahoo! has a patent on the bid-for-placement system that Google licenses for use with AdWords; see www.memwg.com/yahoo-patent for the details.

Second, advertisers pay premium prices to Yahoo! to be shown on large sites like Yahoo! itself and CNN. As such, the values shown by this tool aren't necessarily reflective of what you'd get for displaying the same ads on your site.

Really, the tool is best used to judge the *relative* worth of different keywords. If you want more accurate estimates of pay-per-click values for AdSense ads, use AdWords.

Google AdWords

Seeing what AdWords charges an advertiser for a given keyword is more accurate because the ads displayed by the AdSense program come from the AdWords ad pool and the AdSense fees paid to publishers are a percentage (the exact amount isn't disclosed by Google) of the AdWords fees charged to advertisers. It takes more work to get the values, however, because the information is only available to those who sign up for an AdWords account.

To see what advertisers are currently paying for keywords, you'll need to apply for an AdWords account (`www.memwg.com/adwords`). To sign up, you go through the process of building an ad campaign, which isn't a complicated process. The keyword values are available to you in the second step of the process, after which you simply abandon the application. (Since you're not advertising, there's no need to actually join the AdWords program—you're just looking for keyword values.)

The process is straightforward. First, create an *ad group* by choosing the languages and locations you want to target (**Figure 3.3** and **Figure 3.4**). For Claude and Anita, I chose the English language and all countries. Next, assign a name to your ad group and create a dummy advertisement (**Figure 3.5**). Be sure to enter short phrases (watch your spelling) in the title and description boxes and valid URLs (use www.google.com for simplicity) in the other two boxes. Next, assign keywords to the ad group (**Figure 3.6**).

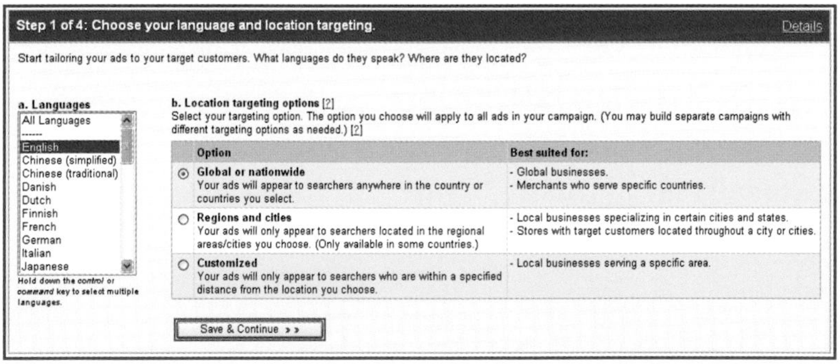

Figure 3.3 Creating a language ad group in AdWords.

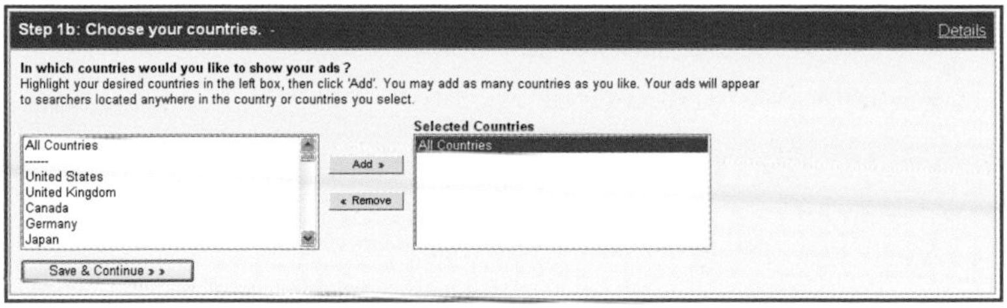

Figure 3.4 Choosing countries in which to display your ad group in AdWords.

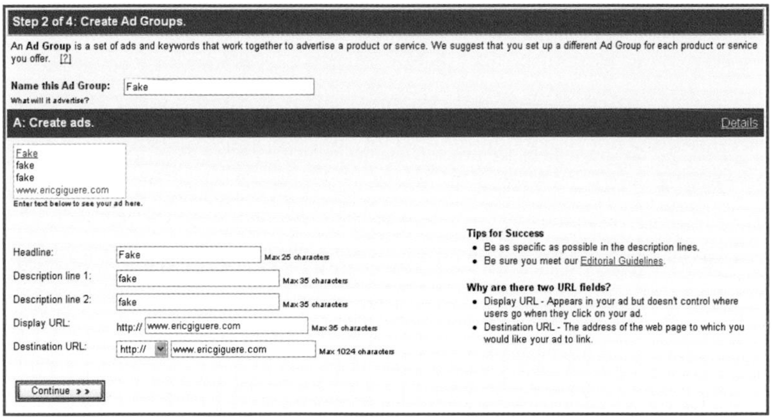

Figure 3.5 Creating a dummy AdWords advertisement.

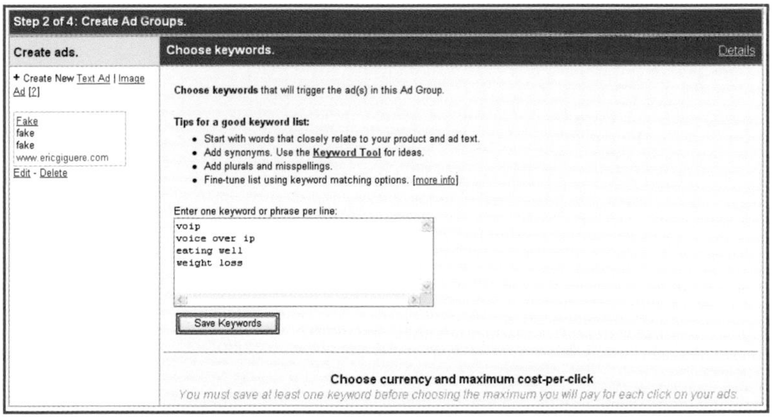

Figure 3.6 Choosing keywords.

For my friends, I entered the following keywords:

▶ voip

▶ voice over ip

▶ eating well

▶ weight loss

This finally brings you to the AdWords Traffic Estimator page (**Figure 3.7**), which lists the average cost per click for each keyword you've chosen. Adjust the maximum cost per click value to $100 (AdWords won't allow you to pay more) and click the Recalculate Estimates button to revise the averages and show what the highest-paying advertisers are being charged (on average) for those keywords.

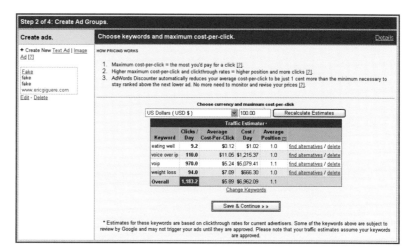

Figure 3.7 The AdWords Traffic Estimator page.

Claude, Anita and I actually spent quite a bit of time playing with the traffic estimator. You can easily change keywords and the estimator will suggest alternative keywords for you if requested. It's actually a lot of fun to do, but take the results with a grain of salt:

Again, we're talking *average* pay-per-click values, most of which are coming from ads shown on Google's own results pages. And it doesn't matter how well-paying the ads are—if no one's visiting your site, you won't make any money.

More Keywords

See www.memwg.com/high-paying-keywords for more information on keywords that can potentially yield significant income.

High-Paying Keywords

Everyone who asks me about AdSense wants to know what the highest-paying keywords are, the ones that pay dollars—or even tens of dollars—per click. Here are some keywords that have paid well in the past:

- mesothelioma
- domain name
- consolidate loans
- credit repair
- line of credit
- web hosting
- voip phone service
- free online poker
- cheap domain

The first keyword—mesothelioma—refers to a type of lung cancer caused by prolonged exposure to asbestos particles. It's the subject of extensive (and expensive) litigation, but it's such a specialized topic that it's doubtful you could make money with it. The other keywords represent more conventional topics. Please remember that this list is just an example and likely will not be current by the time you read it, so see www.memwg.com/high-paying-keywords for a more current list.

Keyword Software

Several companies offer commercial keyword analyzer tools, some with free trial editions. Visit www.Keyword-Toolkit.com, www. WebCEO.com, and www.seo-war.com/ for more.

Other Sources

Various outfits sell lists of top-paying keywords to Web site owners looking for profitable topics. "Buyer beware" is all I'll say—remember that you can determine keyword values for free using the techniques just described.

There are also free lists of keywords available. An often-mentioned list is the one maintained by the 7search.com (`www.memwg.com/7search`) advertising service. This list is pretty much dominated by keywords related to loans and gambling, so it's not that useful. Use these lists as additional sources of information, but be sure to check the values they list with Yahoo! Search Marketing or AdWords.

Assess the Competition

Once you've found a potential topic for your site, assess the competition to see what you're up against. A few Google searches using topic keywords should give you a rough estimate of how many sites already exist. Visit the top-ranked sites and ask yourself these questions:

▶ Does it make sense to build another site devoted to the same topic?

▶ What's going to be new/fresh/unique about your site?

▶ Will visitors find your site?

▶ How will you promote your site?

If the competition is already intense for a given topic, you may want to reconsider your choice of topic. Or narrow your focus and be the big fish in a small pond.

Creating the Content

After spending a good half-hour looking up keyword values, it was time to refill our coffees and talk about some other things. While

Claude went to get our order, I asked Anita if she was still happy with her topic selection.

"Oh, sure," she said. "I know that eating well and exercising isn't exciting. If I was doing it for the money, I'd be better off targeting one of the fad diets. Or something techie—Dad's topic seems to pay well."

"It does for now," I agreed, "because it's new and phone service is something everyone can relate to. But these things change over time; in a couple of years the payouts for voice-over-IP will probably be smaller and your dad will be looking for something better."

Claude had returned with our coffees. "And what's wrong with that?" he said, having overheard me.

"Nothing!" I said. "And over time as your site gains more content you can usually spend less and less time working on it, although a blog isn't so easy to let slide."

"But what do we do now?" Anita asked.

"Now that you've chosen your topic, you can start creating the content for your site."

Claude was surprised. "But I don't have a site!" he protested.

"Not yet, no," I said, "but you have a topic. That's enough to get started. And while you're creating content, there are other things you can do at the same time. Like finding a domain name. But I'll save that stuff for later, when Stef's with us again. Ultimately, it's the content that attracts visitors to your site, directly or indirectly."

"What do you mean?" Anita asked.

"Direct visitations occur when other sites link to yours or through word of mouth from previous visitors," I explained. "High rankings in search engines and web directories are indirect causes of visitation. If you have compelling content and you do some basic promotion of your site, you'll get some traffic."

Writing Guides

A concise writing guide can be found at www.plainenglish. co.uk/reportguide.html. More detailed guidance is available at http:/ /webster.commnet.edu/ grammar/.

"And the more traffic you get," Claude interrupted, "the more chance that your ads will be clicked and the more money you'll make."

"So first we design our Web sites?" Anita asked.

"No, not yet," I said. "Don't confuse content creation with site design. We'll tackle site design later, after you've registered names for your sites and found hosting services to run them for you. But there's no point in doing any of that until you're ready to build some Web pages. Which means creating, gathering, and organizing material for the site."

"You sound like my old English teacher," Claude protested. "I finished school a *long* time ago, you know."

"It *is* a bit like going back to school," I confirmed, "but don't worry—nobody's going to grade you on this stuff."

Dusting Off Old Skills

One of the things you learned in school was how to write essays and reports. You had to research (find, read, and analyze) source documents. You had to form your own thoughts on the topic and put them on paper in logical sequences. You had to check your spelling and use good grammar. You had to reference other people's ideas.

Guess what? You use those *same* skills to create the content for your Web site or blog. A single-topic site, for example, is like writing a long report, complete with sections (the pages) and a table of contents (the home page). A blog is like writing a series of short essays.

If you find writing a chore, you're probably not thrilled to hear this. Claude certainly wasn't. But you can't just go and grab content from other sites and pretend it's yours; that's illegal and unethical. You have to write your own content.

That's why it's important to choose an interesting topic. Maybe you didn't like writing reports and essays in school because they were never about things that interested you. If the topic interests you, you'll be more motivated to write about it. You'll also write better material!

Finding Source Material

Unless you're *the* expert on a topic, you'll need to start with some source material. Gathering this material is useful for different reasons. First, you can reference the material you find on your own site. You want to present accurate information. Second, it educates you about the topic and informs you enough to write intelligently about it. And third, it never hurts to know what others have already written about the topic, even if you already are an expert.

The first place to find your source material is on the Web, of course, for the following reasons:

▶ **Free and easy.** With a few well-placed queries in Google or some simple scanning of the Open Directory project (www.memwg.com/open-directory), you'll find all kinds of topical sites with free information.

▶ **Linkable.** If the information is freely available on the Web, you can easily link to it from your own site. (Links are, of course, *de rigueur* in blogs.)

Losing Visitors to Other Sites

Linking is a two-edged sword, because while it gives your site additional credibility, it also makes it easier for visitors to leave your site. This is how the Web works, though, and you shouldn't fight it. It's also how AdSense works—if a visitor clicks on an AdSense link, they leave your site. Yes, you don't get paid when visitors leave your site via a non-AdSense link, but if your site is well designed and informative, chances are they'll be back. Links are also important to have for page-ranking purposes, as we'll see later.

Amazon Associates

If you cite many books on your site, consider joining Amazon's Associate program—it may generate additional income from your site. Learn more at www.amazon.com/.

On the other hand, there are downsides to using Web-based material:

▶ **Uneven quality.** Some of the information you'll find will be of dubious quality, so be critical in your assessment of its worth. This is especially true of user-contributed encyclopedias and directories like Wikipedia.

▶ **Pages disappear.** Web pages can disappear at any time, temporarily or permanently, which is particularly frustrating when your own pages are linked to them.

▶ **Not everything is free.** High-quality material is often available only to paying users. It's common to put abstracts and summaries up on the Web for free but to require a payment to see the actual article or report.

Sources of information other than the Web should also be considered. Books and articles are obvious choices, and they'll often lead you to still other sources. Talking to and getting advice from knowledgeable people is another possibility—it doesn't cost you anything to send a polite email to an expert, and the chances are good that you'll get some kind of response.

Organizing the Material

After researching the topic, organize the material into meaningful chunks. How you do this depends on whether you're creating a blog or a conventional Web site.

Blogs naturally organize information by date, so one approach is not to do any further organization. As your blog grows in size, though, visitors will have a harder time finding the information they want. Since you can categorize entries on most blog systems, you should decide what the initial set of categories will be and write your first group of blog entries accordingly.

Conventional sites can organize their material however they see fit. Usually there's a home page—the main entry point into the site— and a menu or navigation bar that guides visitors through the major sections of the site. Folders are often used to represent the different sections. We'll look at different strategies for site layout and navigation in chapter 5.

Generally speaking, online material should be organized into smaller chunks than printed material to minimize scrolling. This leads to more pages on your site. Use clearly marked links to ensure that visitors can move easily from one chunk to the next. But don't make the chunks *too* small, or AdSense won't be able to accurately determine what the page is about.

Don't forget, though, that visitors often don't visit your site in an orderly or linear fashion. People often jump into the middle of a site directly from a page of search-engine results, for example. Keep your pages short, but provide context for the visitor who lands on a page without having seen any other page on the site. Make it easy to jump to the home page, for example.

Editing Your Text

Do you know how to spell? Do you have good grammar skills? It's absolutely essential that you write clearly and correctly, no matter what language your site or blog uses. A hard-to-read site doesn't invite repeat visits. Bad grammar and poor spelling also make the site look unprofessional. That's not to say that you can't use slang or acronyms or casual language, but you need to have a good reason to deviate from normal, everyday language use. Writing good content takes time and effort, but it'll be worth it in the long run.

That said, there are sites that deliberately misspell words in order to attract additional search-engine traffic, especially for words that are easily or commonly mistyped. Advertisers also routinely use

Free Text Editors

Need a free text editor? Two popular options are EditPad (www. editpadpro.com/ editpadlite.html) and Cream (http://cream. sourceforge.net/).

misspelled words as keywords for their ad campaigns. It's not an approach I recommend for anyone setting up a site, however.

If you're not confident about your own language skills, there are many free spelling and grammar tools available. See www.memwg.com/spelling-tools for a list. Note that Google can be used for quick spelling and dictionary checks. Misspell a word in a search query, for example, and Google offers the correct spelling as an option (**Figure 3.8**). Definitions for each word in a query are also easily accessed (**Figure 3.9**).

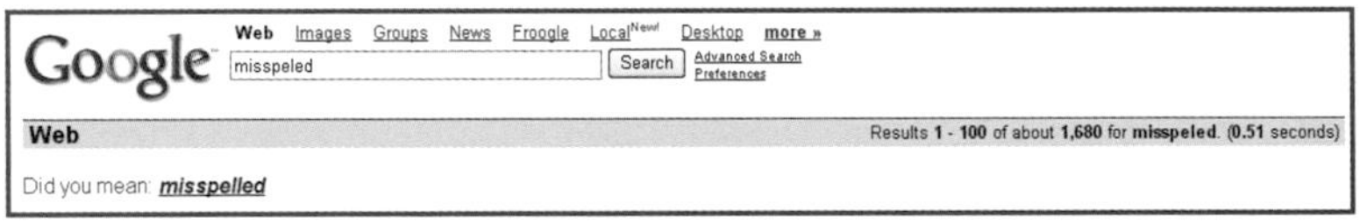

Figure 3.8 Google catches misspelled words.

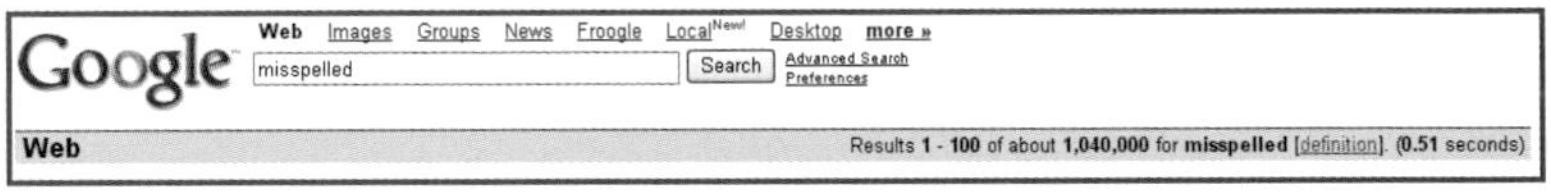

Figure 3.9 Word definitions available from Google.

Add Images and Illustrations Later

AdSense works by analyzing the *text* of a page. Google's computers can't meaningfully interpret images the way a human can, so images by themselves have no bearing on the ads that get shown on a page. You can associate some descriptive text with an image to help Google make sense of it, but in general it's the words on the page that are important. Any images and illustrations you place on the page are mostly there to benefit the human reader. Don't worry too much about these when you first build your site, because you can always add them later.

Plagiarism and Copyrights

Copying someone else's work and passing it off as your own is called *plagiarism*. Plagiarism is a big problem on the Web, and it's something to avoid on your own site. Not only because it's unethical—you're profiting from someone else's hard work without their permission—but also because it's illegal.

Copyright Info

Two useful sites on copyright are "10 Big Myths About Copyright" by Brad Templeton (www.templetons.com/ brad/copymyths.html) and the U.S. Government's pages on copyright law (www.copyright.gov/help /faq/).

Finding Plagiarism with Google

Google makes it easy to find sites that plagiarize. If you think a text is plagiarized, enter a phrase from the text into Google. Be sure to surround the phrase with quotation marks, as this tells Google to treat the words as a single unit instead of as individual words. You'll quickly be able to tell if the phrase was plagiarized or not. College and university instructors regularly use this technique to catch cheaters.

Generally speaking, only the author of an original written work has the right to use and exploit the work. This is the "right to copy," from which the term *copyright* is derived. It's actually a comprehensive set of legal rights, such as the right to publish the work in any form or the right to translate the work into other languages. The owner of these rights—the copyright holder, which is usually the author but could be someone who bought, inherited, or otherwise acquired the copyright—can sell or license the rights to others. Book authors, for example, license their work to book publishers. The publishers then edit, print, distribute, and sell the books on behalf of the author. Without copyright protection, anyone could steal the product of another person's intellectual effort and profit from it.

Copyright does not protect a work indefinitely. Different jurisdictions have different rules, but it's not uncommon for copyright protection to last for fifty or seventy years beyond the author's life-time. If a corporation or some other entity is considered to be the author, copyright protection normally lasts for fifty or seventy years after the work was created. These are just guidelines, because the rules are actually quite complex and depend on when and where the work was created as well as who created it.

Most works today—and this includes the text on a Web page—are protected by copyright, even if there is no copyright declaration shown on the work itself. Copyright protection is implicit and occurs as soon as the work is created. No registration with a government agency is required. (But be sure to consult with a qualified legal professional in your area for all the details.)

When the term of a copyright elapses, the work that was protected by the copyright is said to fall into the *public domain*. A work in the public domain can be used by anyone for any purpose, without any restrictions or payment. Sometimes authors of copyrighted works relinquish their rights and place the works in the public domain prematurely, before the copyright expires. Sometimes works fall into the public domain by statute. Works created by the United States federal government (but not state and local governments) are normally in the public domain, for example, but there are exceptions.

Note that a work can fall into the public domain in one jurisdiction while still being protected by copyright in another. The novel *Gone with the Wind* entered the public domain in Australia in 1999, but it's still protected by copyright in the United States, which caused the operators of Project Gutenberg some grief when they made the text available via their Australian site (see www.memwg.com/gone-with-the-wind). The global reach of the Internet may expose you to legal liability if you use copyrighted works in your material. Unless you're absolutely sure that a work is in the public domain, you must obtain the permission of the copyright owner to include the work on your Web site. Your best defense is to avoid problems by not including anyone else's material on your site (just link to it) and to write all content yourself.

Fair Use

You may be able to quote parts of a copyrighted work under the so-called fair use doctrine, but "fair use" varies on a case-by-case basis. See www.memwg.com/fair-use for more information.

A License to Share

The owner of a copyright has exclusive control over what happens to the work that the copyright protects. Normally, these rights are used to *restrict* what happens to the work. For example, you can't make a copy of most copyrighted works without paying a fee. However, a copyright owner may choose to *freely share or distribute* the work under certain conditions. Most open source software—not just the documentation, but the source code for the software, which is itself a copyrightable work—is shared in this manner, using licenses based on the fundamental rights that copyright owners have to do what they please with their own works. Written works are also being released using this model. For more information on this topic, see www.memwg.com/license-to-share.

Digesting It All

Our coffee cups were empty again. Anita had a few more questions about copyrights, but after answering them I indicated it was time to wrap things up.

"We should meet again soon," I told them, "because there are other things you should be doing while you're thinking about your topics and gathering content."

"Is this where it gets techie?" Anita asked, a bit wary.

"A bit, I suppose," I answered, "but not that much. Like I keep telling you, the concepts are easy. I'll bring my laptop again so we can try a few things out, though."

Claude said he'd see when Stef was available and let me know when they could meet again. The two of them left the coffee shop in quiet conversation. They didn't eat any food, but they had a lot to digest.

chapter four

Getting Ready to Say It

> Stef: I need to move my blog. A friend set it up for me as a favor, but I can't always access it when I want to and sometimes the system goes down.

> Eric: It definitely sounds like you don't control the blog to the extent you should. And what's going to happen to it at the end of the school year when you all leave the dorm? You're right, you should move it. I can help you with that, but before we move it, why don't you join us at our next session.

> Stef: We're going to talk about naming and hosting Web sites and other related things. It'll be useful stuff for you to learn, because ultimately it's about getting and keeping control of your Web presence, whether it's a blog or a standard Web site.

Stef phoned me shortly after my session with Claude and Anita. "I need to move my blog," she said, obviously frustrated. I asked her why she wanted to move it. "Because," she answered, "I want more control over it."

It turns out that the blog was running on a computer in her friend John's dorm room. "He set it up for me as a favor," she said, "but I can't always access it when I want to. Or his system goes down— last weekend we lost power for an hour in the dorm. He was away at his parents' house, though, so my blog was down until he came back and restarted his computer."

"Why didn't he use a blogging service instead of hosting it on his own computer?" I asked.

"He wanted to learn how to set up a blog, I guess," she said. "He's kind of a geek." Realizing to whom she was talking, her tone turned apologetic. "Not that being a geek is bad, of course! I didn't mind it at first when I was learning to blog, but now it's more trouble than it's worth."

"It definitely sounds like you don't control the blog to the extent you should," I agreed. "And what's going to happen to it at the end of the school year when you all leave the dorm? You're right, you should move it. I can help you with that, but before we move it, why don't you join us at our next session. Your dad was going to invite you anyway."

"Are you going to talk about blogs?" she asked.

"Only indirectly. We're going to talk about naming and hosting Web sites and other related things. It'll be useful stuff for you to learn, because ultimately it's about getting and keeping control of your Web presence, whether it's a blog or a standard Web site." Stef agreed to come and said she'd arrange things with Claude.

We all met the next Saturday afternoon at Anita's house. Her husband had taken the children to visit their grandmother, so the house was quiet and Anita seemed quite relaxed.

"As I told Stef," I began, "today we're going to talk about naming and hosting your sites."

It's All About Control

"I have a question," Claude began. "Why can't I just use the free Web space my Internet service provider gives me? They claim it's all that most people need, and they even give me unlimited storage for pictures. Or couldn't I set up a Web server on my own computer, the way Stef has?"

"My blog's not running on *my* computer," Stef objected.

"I know," Claude replied, "but you're not paying to have it run. Seems like a pretty good deal to me."

"Except that she doesn't really control her site," I said. Stef and I described the problems she'd been having with the current system. "Don't forget," I added, "that you're going to be running what is effectively a business, whether you think of it that way or not. Do you really want it controlled by someone who's not accountable to you?"

"But it's free!" Claude asserted again.

"Not really," I explained, "because it costs you time and effort to run and maintain the Web server. In any case, running a Web server on your home Internet connection likely violates the terms of service you agreed to when you signed up for the connection. You'd have to upgrade to a business plan, but it'll cost you more."

"But if they provide free Web space you can use," Anita said, "how is that any different?"

Finding Domain Names
Good places to search for domain names are www.networksolutions.com, www.register.com, and www.web.com.

Domain Name Prices
Check www.buydomains.com and www.dynonames.com for low-cost domain names.

"It's very different because that free Web space is on a Web server in a dedicated data center, monitored and maintained by professionals."

"But you still get your own Web site," Anita maintained.

"Yes," I agreed, "but it'll have an ugly Web address based on your account name. And the size of your site will be limited. More important, the *bandwidth*—the amount of data transferred from your Web site to the browsers accessing it—is likely capped, so if too many people access your site they'll eventually get a message saying that the site's exceeded its bandwidth and to come back next month."

"So how do we get started, then?" she asked.

"You start by getting a Web address for your site," I answered, "and you do that by buying a domain name."

How Domain Names Work

"Is that hard to do?" Anita asked.

"The buying is easy, actually," I replied. "The hard part is *finding* the domain name in the first place. A few years ago, domain names were hot properties that sometimes sold for astronomical amounts. In 1999, for example, the business.com domain sold for $7.5 million, a huge price by any measure."

"Um, that's a bit out of my price range," Claude said quietly.

"Yeah, especially when you're a poor college student," Stef added.

"Don't worry," I assured them. "The dot-com boom fueled an incredible frenzy for high-visibility domain names, but the frenzy died when the boom went bust. You can actually buy a domain name for less than $10 these days. The problem is *finding* a name that somebody else doesn't already own. But we'll get to that later. First, we need to understand how domain names work."

What's a Domain Name?

Every computer on the Internet has a numeric address called an *IP address* (**Figure 4.1**). IP stands for "Internet protocol." The Internet uses IP addresses to route data between computers. The routing can be done very efficiently because it's all based on numbers and computers excel at processing numbers.

Explaining IP

Find a more detailed definition of the Internet Protocol address system, plus check your own IP address, at http:// ipaddr.net/.

Figure 4.1 Example of an IP address for a Web site.

Humans work better with names and symbols than numbers. While IP addresses are very practical and functional at the network level, they're not easily remembered. That's why *domain names* were created. As I explained to Claude before, a domain name is a public, human-readable name for a computer or a group of computers. When you type the name of a Web site into your browser, the browser uses the domain name to find the site's IP address. If I were to make an analogy to the public telephone system, I'd say that a domain name is like an entry in a telephone directory. The system for assigning and resolving domain names is called the *Domain Name System*, or DNS for short.

The Domain Name System delegates authority for managing domain names to different entities on the Internet. This delegation system is reflected in the domain names themselves, which are actually several names glued together (with periods) to form a complete address. In that sense, a full domain name (often referred to as a *fully*

Internationalized Domains

See www.memwg.com/idn for more information about the up- and downsides of using internationalized domain names.

qualified domain name) works much the way a postal address works, except that domain names read left to right instead of top to bottom.

Naming Rules

A valid domain name is almost any combination of English letters (A to Z), numerals, and hyphens. Each individual part of a domain name can be between 2 and 63 characters long. Uppercase and lowercase letters are equivalent, so `www.memwg.com` and `www.MEMWG.com` or even `www.MeMwG.com` all refer to the same domain (**Figure 4.2**).

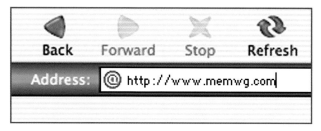

Figure 4.2 Example of a domain name.

Not too long ago, standards were developed to allow letters from non-English alphabets, such as accented French letters or Chinese glyphs, to appear in domain names. Such names are referred to as *internationalized domain names*. The software that runs the DNS cannot directly handle these names, however, and so Web browsers and other applications must encode the internationalized form into a machine-readable equivalent that uses only English characters. We'll stick to English-only domain names to keep things simple.

Top-Level Domains

The name on the extreme right in a full domain name is always a *top-level domain*, or TLD for short. The `.com` domain is the most famous, but today there are many top-level domains in existence.

Each country or territory has its own two-letter domain, for example, such as `.ca` for Canada and `.fr` for France. These are called *country-code* domains. Other top-level domains, like `.info` and `.biz`, are referred to as *generic* domains.

List of Country Codes

Find a list of all the current country codes at www.iana.org/cctld/cctld-whois.htm.

Each top-level domain—also known as a *registry*—is managed by an organization known as the *registry operator*. For country-code domains, the registry operator is often (but not always) a nonprofit organization or government agency. Registry operators for generic domains act under contract with the Internet Corporation for Assigned Names and Numbers (ICANN), the nonprofit corporation that manages the DNS on a worldwide basis (**Figure 4.3**). Only ICANN can authorize the creation of new TLDs.

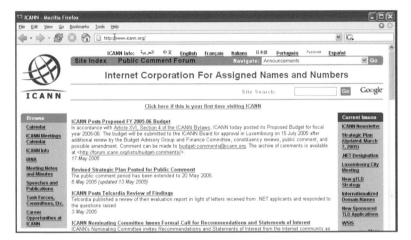

Figure 4.3 The official ICANN Web site.

Subdomains and Host Names

The registry operator maintains the official list of names that are associated with its top-level domain. These names are referred to as *subdomains*, because they are really subdivisions of the top-level domain (**Figure 4.4**). The subdomain is the name found immediately to the left of the top-level domain. (In fact, in a full domain address, any name to the left of another is a subdomain of the latter.) In the domain name `peachpit.com`, for example, `peachpit` is a subdomain of the top-level `.com` domain.

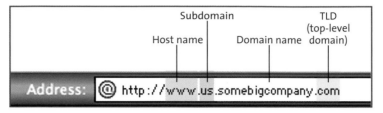

Figure 4.4 Example of a Web address with subdomain.

A subdomain can be further divided, but the registry operator isn't responsible for tracking those subdivisions—it delegates that responsibility to the organization (or individual) that registered the subdomain. A global corporation might subdivide its domain by geography or function, for example, in order to create domain names like `us.somebigcompany.com` or `eng.someothergroup.com`. Each subdomain is listed immediately to the left of its parent domain.

The final part of the full domain name, to the extreme left, is the host name, which identifies a specific computer (by IP address) within a domain or subdomain. Web sites conventionally use `www` as the host name, though any name that follows DNS naming rules is possible. The owner of the domain has complete control over the host names within the domain and over how IP addresses are assigned. Most domains define a default host for the domain, which allows you to drop the host name when browsing—this is why the Web address `http://peachpit.com` gets you to the same site as `http://www.peachpit.com`. The domain owner makes all of this information publicly available on computer systems that the parent domain can access.

In other words, finding the IP address that corresponds to a domain name is a lot like looking through the white pages for a phone number. First you find the right phone book (the top-level domain), then the right city (the subdomain), and then the name of the person or business you want to contact (the host name). This process is called *domain name resolution*, and your computer does it automatically whenever you ask it connect to another computer.

Domain Name Registrars

In DNS parlance, a *registrar* is an organization that can make changes to a domain registry. Its primary function is to register names within a registry. This is a separate role from that of the registry operator, which is charged with *running* the registry. Sometimes the same organization performs both roles—this was certainly the case in the early years of the Internet—but these days registrars are usually separate companies. It's actually a more competitive model, because multiple registrars can be authorized to register names with the same registry. Registrars for generic TLDs are accredited by ICANN, while each national government holds the rights to the accredited registrars for country-code TLDs.

Registrars are businesses. They charge their users—the registrants—a fee for each name registered. The fees are charged on an annual basis: Registrants only rent the names they register, they don't get perpetual rights to them. Parts of these fees go to the registry operator for the maintenance of the registry. The rest is used by the registrar to support itself. The fees charged for domain registrations can vary widely from registrar to registrar, so it pays to shop around to find the best price and the best level of service you're comfortable with.

DNS for Dummies

Learn all about DNS rules and regs at www.yellowclouds.com/DNS.

Accredited Registrars

A list of ICANN-accredited registrars is at www.icann.org/registrars/accredited-list.html. Also see www.memwg.com/registrars for links to popular registrars.

> ## Name Expiration and Renewal
>
> Names are registered for specific time periods like one or two years. At the end of that period, the name is said to expire and it returns to the registry's pool of unregistered names. You must renew a domain registration before it expires in order to guarantee continued rights to the name. Tracking the expiration date isn't usually a problem, because a good registrar will send you a reminder when a domain is about to expire—just don't ignore the reminders!

Note that, at some registries, registrants have to meet certain requirements before they can register a name. The `.name` registry, for example, is restricted to individuals, while the `.pro` registry is restricted to licensed professionals like doctors and lawyers. Country-code TLDs sometimes limit registrations to citizens or organizations of the country in question. Registrars are responsible for enforcing these rules, so be sure to check the rules for the TLDs you're interested in before spending too much time searching for a good name.

WHOIS and Privacy

All information contained in the DNS is public knowledge, including the names and contact information (including email addresses) of domain registrants. An application called WHOIS (a concatenation of "who is") can be used to query this information. Most registrars offer a WHOIS service on their sites (**Figure 4.5**).

If you value your privacy, you may want to take steps to protect or hide your identity when you register a domain name. Spammers monitor new domain registrations to find new email addresses to spam. I've even had hosting services phone me, after I registered a domain, to try to sign me up as a customer.

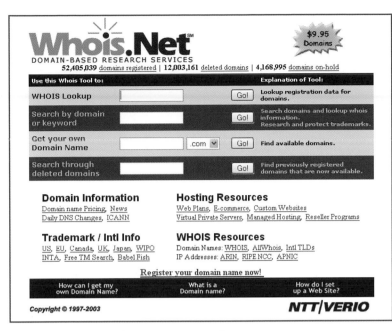

Figure 4.5 A WHOIS domain name search site.

Protecting Your Privacy

Stef was especially concerned about the privacy aspect of registering a domain. "Too many weirdos out there, you know," is how she phrased it. I told her there are steps you can take to protect your privacy:

▶ You can use a different address—Stef could use her father's address, for example.

▶ You can give fake contact information, though the email address needs to be valid.

▶ You can use a privacy service where someone acts as a middleman for you—many domain registrars offer this service.

Just be sure you understand the privacy ramifications of registering a domain name *before* you register.

Finding the Perfect Name

"I like the phone book analogy," said Claude, "but this system seems more complicated."

"Not really," I said. "Have you tried getting a new phone number recently?"

"Yes," Claude answered, "I got a new phone number when I signed up for my residential Internet-based phone service—the voice-over-IP stuff I was talking about earlier."

"So that's the first step—finding a service provider," I continued. "The market's pretty competitive now for any kind of phone service, whether it's wireless or fixed-line. Voice-over-IP adds some interesting twists, though. What area code did you choose for your phone number?"

"The local one," he said. "I didn't have a reason not to."

"You mean he could have chosen a different area code?" Anita asked.

"Sure," I said, "he could have chosen one on the other side of the country, pretty much anywhere the phone company operates. You can do the same with cellphones, too, of course—have them activated in different area codes. That's the second step—choosing the area code."

"That's right," she said, "I remember that. And I even got to choose which cellphone number I wanted from a list of available numbers."

"Exactly," I said, and turned back to Claude. "So you see? Getting a phone number is actually more complicated than you might think at first. Registering a domain name isn't any harder. The hard part is *finding* an unclaimed name, because most of the obvious names are already registered."

"But not all, right?" Stef asked.

"Sometimes you'll be lucky and catch a desirable name immediately after it expires," I agreed, "but that rarely happens. You'll probably have to compromise on the name, but it's worth spending the time to find a good one. You can always change the name later, but things are easier if you start with the best name possible. Let's see how that's done."

Domain Name Spelling
Consider alternate or creative spellings—don't just limit yourself to words in the dictionary. You can use hyphens, capitalization, and other tricks to individualize your name.

List Keywords That Describe Your Site

A domain name is like a brand name for your site. If you've ever tried to name a product or company, you know how hard the process is and how hard it is to find a name that someone else isn't already using. You'll face similar challenges when choosing a domain name. There are no hard rules about what makes a good domain name, but there are some general guidelines to follow: Shorter names are better than longer names, and descriptive names are better than generic names.

The first thing to do is to build a list of keywords that describe your site. Make the list as comprehensive as you can. Include phrases (but no punctuation except for hyphens—no spaces or underscores) in your list. Arrange the list with the names you like best at the top.

Claude's list was as follows:

- voice-over-ip
- voip
- home-phone
- phone-service
- internet-phone
- residential

Anita had different keywords:

- weight
- weight-loss
- eating-well
- nutrition
- exercise

Stef's list was more personal:

- Stef
- college
- life
- random-thoughts
- a-day-in-the-life-of

The lists were actually longer, and I've shortened them for brevity. But be comprehensive with your keyword list.

Trademark Issues

Watch out for trademarks and other protected names. If the name you choose too closely resembles or is easily confused with someone else's intellectual property, they may ask you to stop using the domain name. If you don't, they may start legal proceedings against you and/or use ICANN's domain-conflict resolution process to wrest the domain away from you. See www.memwg.com/domain-name-conflicts for details on the conflict-resolution process.

Select the Top-Level Domains

After building the keyword list, decide which top-level domains to target. Each TLD operates independently, and not everyone who registers a name bothers to register it in every possible TLD. The .com TLD is normally the first choice for a domain name, but it's also the most crowded registry, so you may have better luck finding a good name within the other TLDs.

Which TLD is best? It really depends on your topic and the audience you're trying to reach. Here are the five generic TLDs available to the general public at publication time and what they are (or were) intended for:

- .biz is restricted to business purposes, but there's no strict definition of what constitutes a business.

- .com is unrestricted; it was originally meant for businesses and other commercial entities.

- .info is unrestricted; it was originally meant for making information available to a global audience.

- .net is unrestricted; it was originally meant for Internet service providers.

- .org is unrestricted; it was originally meant for noncommercial purposes.

There are other TLDs, of course, such as the .name and .pro domains I mentioned before, but they're restricted and generally unsuitable for our purposes.

Of the five TLDs above, the .com domain is by far the most common and in many cases the most desirable—a domain ending in .com is instantly recognizable as a domain name. Both Claude and Anita wanted .com domains, if possible. The other four TLDs are about equal in stature. Stef thought .org or even .net suited her needs better than the others.

Generic TLDs

The official list of generic top-level domains is maintained on the ICANN Web site at www.icann.org/ registries/listing.html.

Note that the prices for domains in country-code TLDs are often higher than for those registered in generic TLDs.

What about country-code TLDs? A country-code TLD is a good choice when your topic is specific to a country or language and you meet the TLD's residence requirements, if any. Some of the country-code TLDs have appealing letter combinations: Tuvalu, a former British colony in the southern Pacific Ocean, owns the .tv TLD and generates significant income for itself by selling domain names to television broadcasters.

Multiple Names Are OK

You're not restricted to one domain name for your site or blog. When registering your domain names, check to see if similar names—or the same name in different TLDs—are available, and consider spending the money to register them as well. The same IP address can be associated with multiple names, the same way that married couples with different surnames have separate listings in the phone book for the same phone number. Your Web hosting provider can easily set this up for you. For example, the companion site for this book can be reached from any of the following domain names:

▶ make-easy-money-with-google.com

▶ make-easy-money-with-google.net

▶ MakeEasyMoneyWithGoogle.com

▶ MakeEasyMoneyWithGoogle.info

▶ memwg.com

If you register multiple names, choose one of them as your site's primary name and use it consistently in all links and references to the site, unless you have good reason to use one of the other names. For example, I use the memwg.com name within this book because it makes for shorter Web addresses on the printed page, not because it's the best name for the site.

Choose One or More Registrars

With the TLDs in mind, find an appropriate registrar to work with. Most `.com` registrars can also handle the other four public TLDs, but you may have to use different registrars for the country-code or restricted TLDs.

There's no magic formula to choosing a registrar (**Figure 4.6**). Price is the most important factor to consider. After making sure the registrar can handle the desired TLDs, check out the registrar's price list. Not only do prices vary widely from registrar to registrar, they also vary widely from TLD to TLD within the same registrar. At the time I write this, for example, a `.com` domain sells for $7.95 at many (but not all) registrars, while a `.info` domain sells for as little as $1.95. If you buy domains in bulk—which you won't be doing—you can get even cheaper pricing.

Figure 4.6 A domain-name registrar will offer a variety of services, such as Web hosting, in addition to basic name registration.

Registrar Ratings

See www.memwg.com/
registrar-ratings for links
to different registrar-
rating services.

As with any service, customer satisfaction varies widely among registrars. Some registrars try to lock you into their service by making it hard to transfer your domains to other registrars. Most try very hard to get you to buy their other services, such as Web hosting. (It works both ways, actually, since many hosting services offer domain name registration services as well.) Some don't answer the phone if problems arise. As usual, word of mouth is a good way to go: If you have friends who've registered domain names, ask them whom they recommend.

Not all registrars are directly accredited with ICAAN. Many accredited registrars resell their services to other companies and individuals who want to sell domains but don't or can't meet the stringent accreditation requirements. These services are often rebranded so that you don't know who the true registrar is, and you may pay a higher price for using such a registrar. It's worth digging around a bit to figure out if you're getting a good deal or not.

Search for an Available Domain

Searching for an available domain is easy once you've selected a registrar—just type the desired name into a search box on the registrar's home page (**Figure 4.7**). If it's available, the registrar considerately offers to register it for you; otherwise, the registrar usually suggests alternative names or TLDs to consider instead (**Figure 4.8**).

Figure 4.7 A domain-name registrar's search engine.

Search Results
Check boxes to add domains to your cart.

47 results	pg 1 of 1	50 ⌄ per pg.	back | next	pg.	1 ⌄

add domain	watch list	status
☐ bigmoney.com	🔖	TAKEN
☐ bigmoney.net	🔖	TAKEN
☐ bigmoney.org	🔖	TAKEN

Figure 4.8 Many desirable domain names are not available.

Online Thesaurus

Need an online thesaurus? Try www.m-w.com/, www.thesaurus.com, or www.visualthesaurus.com.

The search process takes time, so don't feel rushed into taking a name that isn't perfect. It helps to have a thesaurus or dictionary on hand to help you with your search in case none of the names on your original list are available. Try prefixing names with articles (*the*, *a*, or *an*) or common adjectives. Try different verb tenses. Be creative!

We went to the computer and tried finding a name for Anita's site first. It was no surprise to any of us that the domains based on her keyword list were all taken—they were all common words. Then we tried some variations, but nothing was available except names like `WeightLossAnita.com` that didn't appeal to her at all. After scratching our heads for a while, I asked Anita what her site's main focus was—weight loss or nutrition.

"It's both," she said, "because I really believe they go hand in hand. Eating well leads naturally to weight loss."

"Then let's find you a domain name that includes both concepts of *eating well* and *weight loss*," I told her, resuming the search. In the end, we came up with the name `EatLessWeighLess.com`, which Anita thought was a good description of her philosophy.

Claude asked me whether hyphens in domain names were a good idea. "Shouldn't she use `Eat-Less-Weigh-Less.com` instead?" he wondered.

VOIP

For more on voice-over-IP, see the links at www.voip-at-home.com/.

I described the pros and cons of hyphenated domain names. The advantages are that hyphenated names are easy for humans to read without resorting to capitalization tricks and that search engines can easily split the name into separate keywords. The disadvantages are that hyphenated names are longer, harder to type, and easily confused with their unhyphenated equivalents.

"Ideally," I said, "you'd grab both the hyphenated and unhyphenated versions of the same name and have them both point to your Web site."

Anita wasn't interested in the hyphenated version, though. "Maybe later," she said, "but one's enough for now."

For Claude, however, I thought a hyphenated name might make a lot of sense. The problem with his site was that neither the phrase *voice-over-IP* nor the acronym *voip* are common English terms, especially the latter. Any name that included *voip* in it would be clearer in its hyphenated form, I thought, and Claude agreed. Since Claude was going to focus on residential uses of VoIP technology, we started by looking at names that included both *voip* and *home* in them. In the end, Claude chose `voip-at-home.com` as his domain name. "I think it's pretty clear what the site's about if they know what the *voip* stands for," he said, and I agreed.

Stef's name was the last to be chosen, but it was the easiest to find because she absolutely wanted "Stef" in the name and she wasn't interested in the `.com` top-level domain. Her existing blog was called "Stef at College," so that's what we started with. As it turned out, `Stef-at-College.org`, `StefAtCollege.org`, `Stef-at-College.net`, and `StefAtCollege.net` were all available. I also noticed that the `.com` versions were unclaimed and that she might want to get them anyhow, but Claude pointed out in a very fatherly tone that Stef was a "poor college student" after all and perhaps she should just choose one or two to start with. She chose the two `.org` versions. Now it was time to register everyone's chosen names.

Domain Resellers

See www.memwg.com/
domain-resellers for
details on purchasing
domains from a reseller.

> ## Names for Sale
>
> If the domain name you really want is already registered, you may still be able to obtain it by purchasing it from the person or company who owns it. Type the domain name into your Web browser and see if you land on a "domain for sale" page, which usually leads you to the site of a domain reseller. Alternately, contact the owner of the domain (using the WHOIS information if it's available) and ask if they'd be willing to sell it to you.

Register the Name

We went to a registration site and I walked them through the process. The details vary by registrar, but in general there are four steps to follow:

1. Create an account with the registrar. This is free, but you'll need a valid email address. The account lets you check the status of your registrations as well as make changes later.

2. Grab the domain names and add them to your online shopping cart.

3. Fill in the registrant and contact information for each domain name.

4. Check out and complete the transaction by using a credit card to pay the domain registration fees.

There may be additional steps required at checkout time, such as confirming that you're entitled to register a domain in a particular registry. The registrar will try to sell you additional features or services, such as private domain name registration or Web hosting services. You can decline most of these, except perhaps for the privacy protection if privacy is a concern.

Permanent Email

Get a permanent email address at www.pobox. com, www.hotmail.com, or www.netaddress.com/.

Domain Names and Email Addresses

The contact information for a domain includes email addresses. Those addresses must be valid and regularly monitored, otherwise important notices that the registrar sends you—such as requests by unscrupulous parties to transfer the domain to them—will be lost. Email addresses that are not tied to your school, employer, or Internet service provider are best, otherwise you'll have to remember to change the registration information for each of your domains whenever you change email addresses. Since registrars require domain owners to confirm such changes via email, you'd have to make those changes before you lose the email addresses in question. A "permanent" or "lifetime" email address that you monitor on a regular basis is a good address to use, though expect the amount of spam you receive at that address to increase once the address is made public in the domain registration information.

When you register a domain, you must supply contact information (name, address, phone number, email address) for the owner (you) as well as for the *administrative* and *technical* contacts. You can (and initially should) use the same contact information for all three. The administrative contact receives requests for approval or information when there is an administrative issue with a domain that needs to be addressed by the registrar or by ICANN—for example, the domain is up for renewal. The technical contact is contacted whenever there's a technical problem with the domain. Contact information can be changed at any time.

At some point in the registration process, you'll be asked to provide DNS information for each domain, specifically the IP addresses of the *name servers* for the domain. Name servers are computers that know how to map the host names or subdomains within a domain into actual IP addresses. You don't have this information yet, so choose the free "parking" option to let the registrar temporarily host your domain. While the domain is parked, anyone who enters the domain name into a Web browser is presented with a "coming soon" Web page (**Figure 4.9**).

Registration
Propagation

You own the domains as soon as you pay the registration fees, but it normally takes a few hours for the registrations to take effect, so don't be surprised if your "coming soon" pages aren't shown at first.

Figure 4.9 A sample "coming soon" Web page for a parked domain.

As the owner, you can change the registration information for any of your domains at any time through your registrar's Web site. You can even transfer domains to another registrar or to another person. Important changes like transfers will require confirmation (by email) before they occur.

Lock Your Domains

Some domain owners have had their domain names hijacked from them by unscrupulous individuals who managed to convince a registrar that an owner had authorized a transfer. To combat this, most registrars let you lock your domains at no extra charge to automatically refuse any transfer requests. If you legitimately want to transfer a locked domain, you must first return to the registrar and unlock the domain before proceeding with the transfer. Locking your domains is a good idea.

Hosting the Site

"Wow!" Stef exclaimed, "Now I own two domains. Thanks, Dad!" Claude had paid the registration fees for her domains with his credit card. And except for the name and email addresses, Stef's contact information was identical to Claude's. Anita had used her own address and credit card, of course.

"Now that we've named your sites, we need to host them with a hosting service," I said.

"They'll actually run the Web sites for us, right?" Claude asked.

"Right," I agreed. "They'll also provide email services for your domains."

"But I already have an email address," Claude protested. "In fact, I have several. *Too many*, really. I don't want any more."

"You don't actually have to get a new email address," I explained. "The hosting service can forward mail to one of your existing addresses, so you don't need to create new mail accounts. But normally you *want* to."

"Why is that?" Anita asked.

"For different reasons," I said. "but mostly to look more professional and to protect your personal email address."

"Sounds complicated again," Anita said.

"It's not, but we're getting ahead of ourselves. Email is just one component of what a hosting service offers."

What's a Hosting Service?

Hosting services are businesses that manage Web servers, mail servers, and other Internet-based services. The computers on which the services run are housed in data centers with dedicated high-speed Internet connections and round-the-clock monitoring. Hosting services normally own the hardware in their data centers and charge customers for their use.

A hosting service saves you a lot of work. The hosting service installs and configures the computers and software needed to run your Web site and related services. It's responsible for keeping the system up and running (the industry refers to this as *uptime*) on a continuous basis. It takes care of all the mundane but important details of running a Web site—performing regular backups, maintaining the hardware, monitoring and upgrading the software—that even technically savvy people would be hard-pressed to do on their own.

None of this comes for free, of course, because data centers are expensive to run. Hosting services recover their costs by charging rental fees, generally on a monthly basis. The fees are based on the services required—how much disk space, how much network traffic, which operating system—and can vary widely from hosting service to hosting service. But basic hosting services (bundled together into a *hosting plan*) are available for $5 to $10 a month from a wide variety of vendors.

Choose a hosting service the same way you choose a domain registrar, by comparing prices and services. Like registrars, hosting service providers often resell their services, so it may not be obvious who is the actual service provider.

What To Look For in a Hosting Service

All hosting services are not created equal, so it pays to shop around. But before you do, you need to understand what services are available so you can choose the monthly hosting plan that's right for you.

Free Hosting

Some hosting services will host your site for free if you're willing to let them display ads on your site. But it's best to stay away from the free services and pay a small fee to get total control over your site.

Rating Hosts

Ratings of hosting services can be found at www.memwg.com/hosting-service-ratings.

Web Site Hosting

Hosting Web sites is a hosting service's primary business, so you should carefully look over the features each service offers before making your decision (**Figure 4.10**). Initially, your needs will be very simple—the most basic hosting plan a service offers is good enough in most cases—but it's important to leave yourself room to upgrade the services later if necessary.

Figure 4.10 The home page of OCHosting, a hosting service based in California.

There are three basic types of Web site hosting:

▶ With *shared* or *virtual hosting*, several (often many) independent sites share the same computer.

▶ With *dedicated hosting*, you rent the exclusive use of a computer for your site (or sites).

▶ With *co-located hosting*, you actually own the computer (either you buy it from the hosting service or else you ship it to the service's data center) and the hosting service manages it for you.

Both dedicated and co-located hosting are costly. Shared hosting, however, can be had fairly cheaply because the hosting service can spread the cost of maintaining the hardware across a whole slew of separately owned Web sites. Shared hosting is what you'll start with, so ignore any dedicated or co-located hosting plans.

The actual server computer that hosts the Web sites runs an operating system, of course, just like any other computer. Most hosting services run Linux-based computers. Linux is free and is well suited to running Web servers. Some services are exclusively Windows-based. Some support both operating systems and let you choose the one that best suits your needs. A few hosting services run other operating systems like FreeBSD and OpenBSD. For basic Web sites, the kind you'll create, any of these operating systems will do.

The Web server software itself is actually more important than the operating system it's running on. Most Linux-based sites run the Apache HTTP Server, a free Web server, and most Windows-based sites run Internet Information Services (IIS for short), a Microsoft product. Although all modern Web servers work the same way and provide the same basic features, how you configure and manage the server depends on the software used. For example, Apache and IIS have different ways of password-protecting parts of a Web site. In most cases, however, an Apache-based server is the simplest to work with.

BSD

Go to www.netbsd.org/Documentation/bsd/ for more info on BSD.

Free Web Servers

See www.memwg.com/apache for more on the Apache free Web server, and www.memwg.com/iis for more on Microsoft's Internet information Service.

The Control Panel

Note that most hosting services provide you with a control panel for monitoring and managing your Web site (**Figure 4.11**). The control panel lets you control the major aspects of the Web site remotely from any browser.

Figure 4.11 An example of a control panel from the site management page provided by OCHosting.

When you choose a hosting plan, pay careful attention to the monthly *bandwidth* and *disk space* limits of the plan. Bandwidth refers to the amount of data transferred across the network to and from your Web site. Every time someone accesses your Web site, it uses up some of your bandwidth. Disk space is the amount of storage available to you on the server computer; the larger your site, the more storage you'll use. If you exceed either limit, the hosting service will charge you extra fees that month. For a simple site, basic limits of 1 GB of bandwidth and 25 to 50 MB of disk space are quite adequate to start with, but if you find yourself exceeding these on a regular basis, you should consider upgrading to a different plan with higher limits.

Email Services

Email services come free with most Web hosting plans. In other words, the hosting service will handle mail sent to and from any domains that you host with them.

The email accounts you get from your hosting service are similar to what you get from your Internet service provider—after all, an ISP offers the same types of services. The hosting service will provide you with an account name and password, as well as the details for setting up your mail client (Thunderbird, Outlook Express, Eudora—any modern mail client that supports multiple email accounts) or using a browser-based mail reader.

Free Email Clients

For more on the Thunderbird mail client, visit www.mozilla.org/products/thunderbird/. For more on Eudora, see www.eudora.com.

Sending Mail

When sending mail related to your Web site, remember to use the email address provided by the hosting service, not your personal address. This is usually done by sending the mail through the hosting service's email (SMTP) server, not through your ISP's. If this capability isn't available, at least configure your mail client to set the "From" and "Reply To" parts of the mail message to the other address in order to mask your personal email address as much as possible.

Basic hosting plans normally come with just a few email accounts, but most offer the ability to created email *aliases*, email addresses that do nothing but forward the mail they receive to another address. Most plans also have the ability to create a *catchall* alias, an email

FTP for Newbies

A good beginner's guide to FTP can be found at www.ftpplanet.com/ftpresources/basics.htm.

address that "catches" all mail sent to an address for which there is no account or alias. Catchall accounts get a lot of spam, however, so you're better off creating individual aliases and disabling the catchall feature entirely.

Other Services

Besides Web hosting and email, other services may be available:

▶ **Backups.** The service provider should regularly back up your Web site and quickly restore it whenever hardware problems occur.

▶ **FTP support.** Short for File Transfer Protocol, FTP is a standard way to transfer files to and from remote computers. At a minimum, the hosting service will provide you with instructions for using FTP to copy the Web pages you create on your home computer to the server that hosts your actual Web site.

▶ **Shell/Telnet.** Direct access to the Web server is obtained using a shell or telnet account. This is strictly for techies, so don't worry about it.

▶ **Databases.** Large amounts of data are stored and manipulated using databases. Again, this is for techies, as programming is definitely required.

▶ **Forums and Mailing Lists.** These let you communicate with your visitors. Note that a blog may make more sense.

▶ **Shopping Carts and Scripts.** Most hosting services supply pre-written programs that you can use to add shopping carts and other interactive behaviors to your Web site. These all require some programming, however.

Other than backups and FTP support, which are basic services, the services listed above may only be available with the more advanced plans. Some service providers offer various services *à la carte* as well.

Most of these additional services aren't necessary for the kind of Web site you're going to build, so don't buy a premium hosting plan. You can always upgrade your plan later, if necessary.

Signing Up for Web Hosting

Signing up for hosting services is very similar to registering a domain name. After choosing the hosting service, use its Web site to create a new account with the appropriate hosting plan. You'll need a credit card, of course.

After signing up, you'll receive email from the service with important details about your new hosting account, including:

▶ The IP address of the Web server that will host your site. You can use this to temporarily access the site.

▶ The addresses of two name servers that the hosting service controls, to update the DNS information for your domain name.

▶ The URL of the control panel for your Web site, including the account login and password needed to access it.

▶ The addresses of the mail servers, to update your mail client.

Save the email for later reference—you don't want to lose this information. Since your domain is currently parked, head over to your domain registrar's Web site to unpark it. Enter the name server addresses supplied by your hosting service into the appropriate fields in your domain's administration page (**Figure 4.12**). It will take anywhere from a few hours to a couple of days for the information to propagate across the DNS. In the meantime, you can use the IP address supplied by the hosting service (or an alternate Web address that it supplies) to access your site from a Web browser.

Hosting Discounts
Many hosting services offer discounts if you pay for services on a quarterly or annual basis.

Set Name Servers

Apply changes to:

○ Single Domain (MAKE-EASY-MONEY-WITH-GOOGLE.COM)

○ All Eligible Domains

Name Servers control how a domain name is resolved. If you are hosting with GoDaddy.com, just select Default Hosting Name Servers and we will fill in the values for you. Or, if you would like to use one of our Parked Pages until you build a site of your own, click Default Parked Name Servers.

If you will be using other Name Servers, please select Custom Name Servers and enter them in the spaces provided.

Changes to Name Servers may take up to 48 hours to take effect.

○ **Default Hosting Name Servers**

○ **Default Parked Name Servers**

⊙ **Custom Name Servers**

Name Server 1: NS1.KGB.REGINA.SK.CA *

Name Server 2: NS2.KGB.REGINA.SK.CA *

Name Server 3:

*Required field

Add New Nameserver

Save Changes **Cancel Changes**

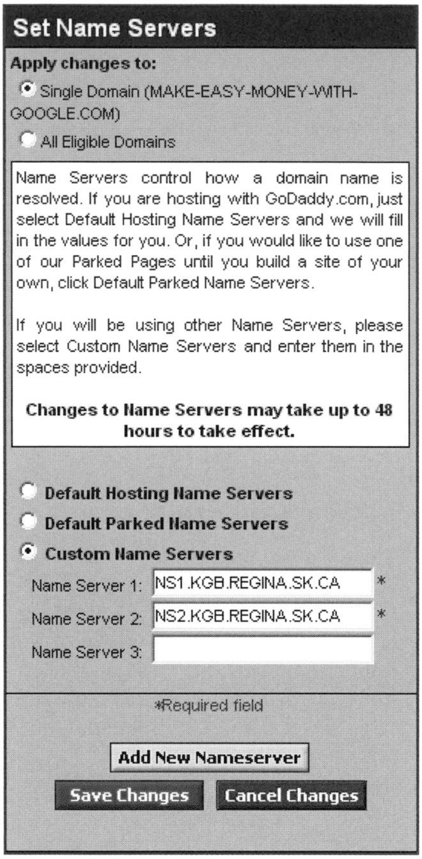

Figure 4.12 Assigning name servers to a domain.

Wait until the DNS has been updated (at which time you can access your new site using its domain name, not just its IP address) to set up your mail client. You won't be able to receive mail until then anyhow.

Explore the control panel to familiarize yourself with its features. For a simple site, there are few things to worry about. You'll use the control panel mostly to create and manage email accounts.

Moving Forward

Stef was surprised to see me shut down my laptop. "Aren't we going to sign up for our hosting services?" she asked me.

I shook my head. "Not yet," I said. "You've got your domain names, which is the important thing—it's important to grab those right away while they're available. The hosting can wait, though, until you have some content for the site."

"Or you want to use your new email address," added Claude.

"That's right," I agreed. "But otherwise, there's no point in doing it yet."

"It's getting late anyhow," Anita said, "the kids will be back shortly."

"You've given us a lot to think about again," said Claude. "What's our next session going to be about?"

"Designing your site," I answered. "We're going to talk about page layout, navigation, and basic Web design principles. Can you all come to my place next time? I'll need a bigger screen to show you some things."

Nobody objected, so we agreed on a time and I left Anita's house just as her husband returned with the children. It had been a long session, but we'd ended it just in time!

section three

Starting

Content

Design

AdSense

Traffic

chapter five

Designing Your Site

> Stef: I hope you don't mind, but I signed up for a hosting service already. I wanted to use my new domain name to send emails. Now I use stef@stefatcollege.org as my main email address.

> Eric: But you haven't moved the blog yet, right?

> Stef: Not yet, no. Is that going to be hard?

> Eric: Yes, it's a little tricky. You'll only do it once, though, so get your friend to help you with that. But now let's discuss today's topic—designing your site.

When the others arrived at my house for our next session, I had moved a computer monitor onto my dining room table so that the three of them wouldn't have to crowd around my laptop. After exchanging the usual pleasantries, Stef made an announcement.

"I hope you don't mind, but I signed up for a hosting service already," she told us.

"Doesn't bother me," I replied. "I hope it was easy to do."

"Signing up was really easy," she explained, "but I made sure my friend was around just in case I had any trouble. I didn't."

"Is this the same friend who currently hosts your blog?" I asked.

"Yes," she said. "I figured I should tell him I was planning on moving the blog off of his computer. He was happy, actually, because he'd been wondering what to do with the blog at the end of the year. He was *very* interested in the AdSense program, too, you know."

"I don't think we have room for another person at the table!" I joked.

"That's OK," she continued, "I think he already knows most of this stuff anyhow, he just never got around to explaining it to me." She seemed a bit peeved.

"You probably didn't show any interest, Stef," said Anita.

"Well," I said, "if he's the geek you say he is, then I'm sure he can figure things out on his own. You can give him my email address in case he has questions. But Google's AdSense help pages are pretty detailed."

"So why did you sign up?" Anita asked. "You don't have any content yet."

"More importantly," Claude interrupted, "how did you pay for it?"

"Well, actually, she does have content," I pointed out in response to Anita's question. "She already has a blog. That's definitely content."

"That's not why I signed up," Stef explained. "I wanted to use my new domain name to send emails. Now I use stef@stefatcollege.org as my main email address. And I found a hosting service that uses PayPal, Dad, so I didn't have to use your credit card. The hardest part was getting my mail software to work once the hosting service had set things up, but the instructions they sent were pretty good."

"But you haven't moved the blog yet, right?" I asked her.

"Not yet, no," she said. "Is that going to be hard?"

"If you want to keep the old content," I started, and she nodded that she did, "then yes, it's a little tricky. You'll only do it once, though, so get your friend to help you with that. But now let's discuss today's topic—designing your site."

Thinking About Design

Claude had a question. "When you say 'design,' do you mean what the site looks like?" he asked.

"Yes," I answered. "What it looks like *and* how it's used—the layout and the navigation."

"Layout I understand," Anita said, "but what do you mean by *navigation*?"

"How you move from page to page within the site," I explained, pointing to a Web page I had up on the monitor. "How you find your bearings within the site. Links, menus, site maps—all that stuff."

Claude was unimpressed. "Surely it's not that hard to do. Can't you just copy someone else's design?"

"Site design can be very hard if you do it from scratch," I said. "You can spend days thinking about and preparing your site. In fact, you can waste a lot of time on the smallest details—trust me, I've done it!

But none of us are professional designers. So yes, Claude, you want to look at what other sites have done and do something similar, though you don't literally *copy* them."

"You can also buy books about Web design and learn from them," Stef said. "My friend has a few of those."

"Absolutely—there's nothing wrong with a good book!" I continued. "I have some I can lend if you're interested, but you can learn a lot just by looking at other sites."

Claude was eager to take me up on the offer. "Do you have a book that shows you how to add blinking text to your site?" he asked.

Now I knew who was going to need the most help! "You know, blinking text isn't a great thing to add to a Web site, Claude," I said gently. "In fact, as a nonprofessional you want to avoid getting too fancy, otherwise your site will look cluttered and confuse your visitors. Better to keep things simple. I'll show you what I mean shortly, but first let's talk about the important parts of a Web site and what kinds of things you need on your pages."

The Components of a Web Site

I turned to the computer and opened a new browser window. "As you can see," I began, "my browser automatically loads the Google search page www.google.com when it starts." They all looked at the big monitor while I was talking (**Figure 5.1**). "This is Google's *home page*. The home page is the Web site's main page, the one that shows up when you enter the site's address in the browser. Every site has a home page."

"It's very simple," Anita said. "I like it a lot."

"Now let's contrast it with Yahoo!'s home page," I said, opening www.yahoo.com (**Figure 5.2**) in a second browser.

Figure 5.1 The Google home page.

Figure 5.2 The Yahoo! home page.

"It's a lot busier," Anita said.

"That's because Google's main focus is its search engine," I explained, "while Yahoo! has a number of businesses to promote. If all you're interested in is searching the Web, Yahoo! has its own search page that is very similar to Google's home page." I had the browser display the Yahoo! search page found at search.yahoo.com (**Figure 5.3**).

Figure 5.3   The Yahoo! search page.

Stef spoke up. "That does look pretty similar!"

I closed the second browser and moved back to the Google home page. "Designing your home page is probably one of the hardest things you'll do," I continued, "because a visitor needs to be able to tell at a glance what the site is about and how to navigate through it. I'm sure you've all come across sites that had hard-to-use home pages."

"Yeah," Claude said, "sometimes they're so confusing I just hit the Back button and move to another site."

"Many sites try to pack too much information on their home page," I agreed. "If you're a big portal like Yahoo! it makes sense—that's really what a portal is, after all—but most sites aren't in that category. Google's minimalist approach is the other extreme. Your site will fall somewhere in the middle."

"So how do you find other pages on the Google site?" Stef asked, pointing to Google's home page.

"You click on the About Google link at the bottom," I said, as I clicked the link. "This brings you to a much busier page." The browser was now displaying the page **www.google.com/about.html** (**Figure 5.4**). "This is a *site map* page. A site map is basically a categorized listing of the site's important pages. It's a navigational aid that visitors can turn to when they don't know where to find something. Not every site needs a site map, but it really helps if you're doing the minimalist approach. The Google page you're looking at is a very basic site map. Oddly enough, Google has a bigger site map that has no link from its home page, though other pages within Google's Web site refer to it." Typing the address **www.google.com/sitemap.html** (**Figure 5.5**) directly into the browser brought up the comprehensive site map.

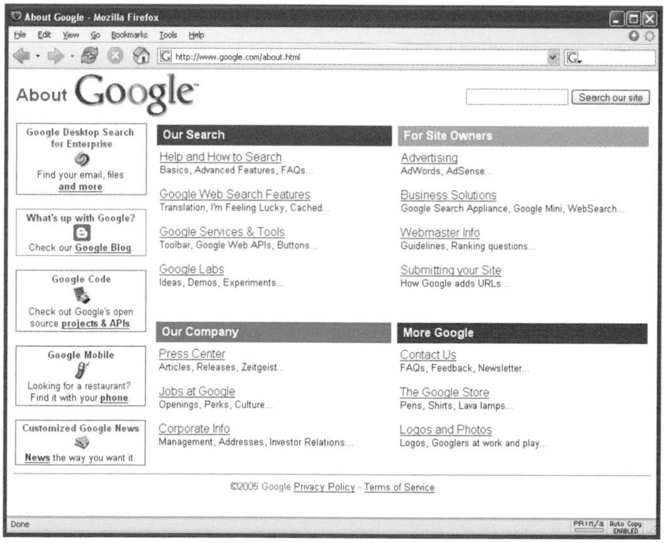

Figure 5.4 Google's basic site map.

Figure 5.5 Google's comprehensive site map.

"What about other page types?" Stef asked again.

"There are no real standards beyond having a home page," I answered, "so it really depends on what kind of site you're building. But there are some common types." I switched the browser to Google's corporate information page, `www.google.com/corporate/index.html` (**Figure 5.6**). "These are Google's *about pages*, which describe the company itself. It's a good idea to have a page that describes what your site is about and how to contact you if there are problems or questions. Another good idea is to include a *search page* to let users find things on the site." I showed them a search page I had developed for one of my sites (**Figure 5.7**). "Google makes it so easy, because as an AdSense publisher you just need to sign up for AdSense for search and put the search code Google generates onto a separate page."

"Or right on each page," Claude interjected.

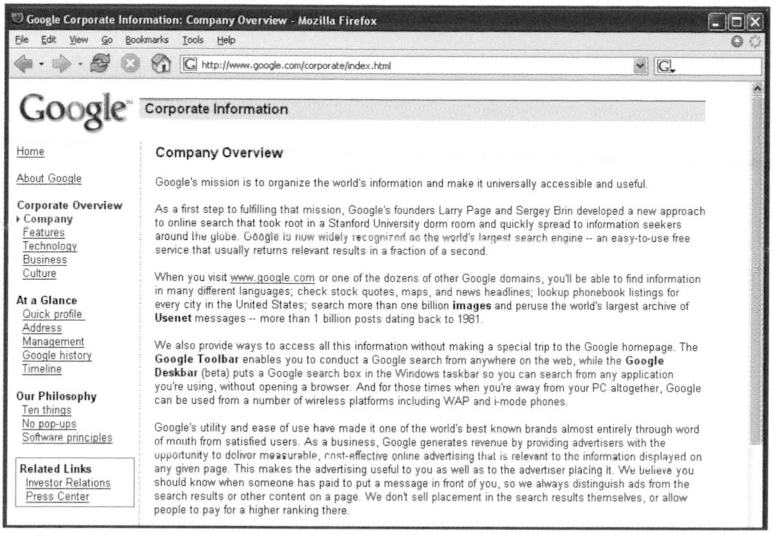

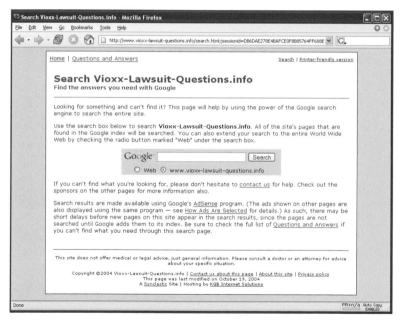

Figure 5.6 Google's corporate information page.

Figure 5.7 A sample search page.

"Yes, if you don't mind losing some screen real estate," I agreed. "Either way works. The important thing is that you have a search facility. Plus, using Adsense for search means you'll probably make some revenue—it's not usually very much—from the searching itself."

"Every little bit helps!" Claude said happily, and I nodded in agreement.

"Beyond those basic pages," I continued, "there are no real rules. It all depends on the kind of site you're building. Some sites include a *what's new* page describing major changes in reverse chronological order, like the one on my personal site." Again I switched the browser, this time to `www.ericgiguere.com/whatsnew.html` (**Figure 5.8**). "Of course, a blog doesn't need a separate page for this—it's implicit in the blog itself."

Anita spoke up. "What about other ways to navigate the site?" she asked. "I don't use site maps and search pages very much."

Figure 5.8 A sample *what's new* page.

"That's a very good question," I answered, "and that brings us to our next topic." All three of them turned away from the monitor and listened carefully as I described how site navigation works.

Site Navigation

A key Web concept is the ability to jump from page to page using links. At its simplest, *site navigation* refers to the links that let visitors move from page to page within your site. But there's more to it than that: It's about making it easy for visitors to find what they're looking for on the site.

Nav Tools Needed

Good site navigation tools are especially useful for visitors who arrive at your site directly from a search engine results page and never even see your home page.

Landing Pages

A *landing page* is any page on your site with a link from another site. Visitors "land" on your site by following those links. The home page is an obvious landing page. Once your site is found by a search engine, though, almost every page becomes a landing page, so good navigational aids are essential on all pages.

Whatever you do, *don't trap visitors on your site* by disabling the browser's Back button or otherwise interfering with their browsing. Besides violating AdSense terms of service, such techniques almost ensure that visitors never come back once they manage to get away from your site.

Let's start with the links. Every page on your site should include links to these pages:

> ▶ **Home page.** Since the home page is the official starting page, make it easy to find with a link called "Home" or "Main Page." Or name it after the site's domain name. (Your site's logo, if you have one, should also link to the home page.)

AdSense Search Box

If you're using AdSense for search as your search facility, you'll have to wait until you're accepted into the AdSense program to add the search box, but you can still create the search page and link to it from the other pages.

▶ **About page.** First-time visitors often want to know more about the site and the people or organization behind it. The about page is also the ideal place to put contact information like email addresses.

▶ **Search page.** Even the most well-organized site benefits from a good search facility, so don't bury it away somewhere. Search boxes can even be placed directly on individual pages for added ease of use.

▶ **Site map page.** The site map gives visitors another way to quickly grasp what your site is about and what it has to offer.

Not only do these links entice visitors to stay, they also make the site look fuller and more professional. Creating these pages is an easy way to test and flesh out the initial look and feel of the site without worrying too much about the content. They'll also improve your chances of being accepted into the AdSense program. Most blogs provide these kinds of pages and links automatically, of course, though they may refer to them by different names.

Search Engines Love Site Maps

Not only are site maps great resources for human visitors, they also let search engines like Google find all the important pages on the site, whether or not the home page links to them. Just make sure the home page links to the site map, and call it "sitemap.html" or some variation thereof so that humans and computers recognize it for what it is. Above all else, though, be sure to update the site map as you add or remove pages to your site!

Your site's pages must also link to each other in predictable ways:

- The first part of an article should link to later parts, and vice versa.
- Long, multipage documents need a separate page for the table of contents.
- If you group pages into sections, there should be a main page for each section that links to each page in the section, and each section page should link back to the main page.
- Related pages should be linked together as well, whether or not they're in the same group.

Note that links can be added to a page at any time, so remember to add or update links as the site changes.

Links can be grouped together. A *navigation bar* lets the visitor quickly navigate the Web site without referring to the full site map. Horizontal navigation bars are usually found at the top (**Figure 5.9**) of the page, while vertical ones are normally found to the left of the page content (**Figure 5.10**).

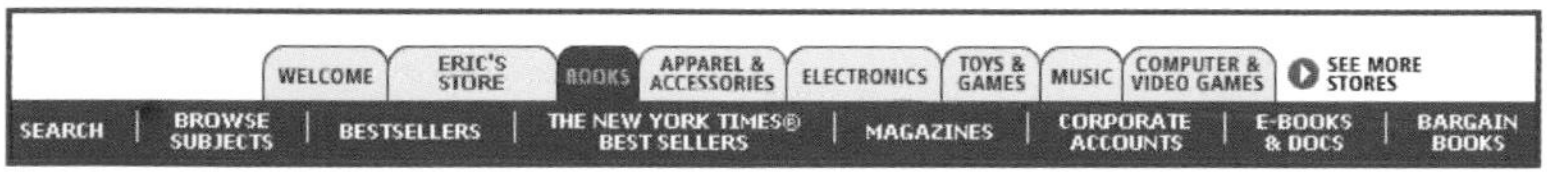

Figure 5.9 A horizontal navigation bar.

Figure 5.10 A vertical navigation bar.

Use Descriptive Links

Strive to be as descriptive as possible with your links. Avoid redundant and generic phrases like "Click here" or "Click for more information," and describe what the target page is about (for instance, "Click to see a map of the campus").

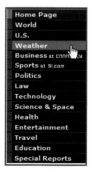

Navigation links are often separate from the page content. Links *in* the content (*inline* links) must be used sparingly, because having many links makes the text harder to read, especially when links are underlined in the traditional manner. Compare a paragraph with a single link in it (**Figure 5.11**) to one with five inline links (**Figure 5.12**). Too many links too close together is just too confusing!

The nice thing about Google's AdSense program is that you can make money with almost no effort. All you need is a Web site and some traffic.

Figure 5.11 A paragraph with a single inline link.

When you go overboard with inline links in your text, you'll find that the paragraph text can be hard to read.

Figure 5.12 A paragraph with five inline links.

Note that site navigation is built around *internal* links—links to other pages on the same site. *External* links—links to other sites—are also important, but they're not involved in site navigation.

Providing Context

Navigational aids work best if visitors have some sense of where they are when they visit your Web site. This is especially true for visitors who arrive at your site without seeing your home page. Providing them with context encourages them to explore your site in more detail.

Context is provided in a number of different ways. These are all small things, but together they provide important navigational clues for your visitors:

▸ **Title.** How many times have you come across an untitled page like the one shown in **Figure 5.13**? Every page on your site needs a title that accurately and concisely describes the page content. And remember that the title is one of the things AdSense uses to determine the page's topic, so include keywords in the title.

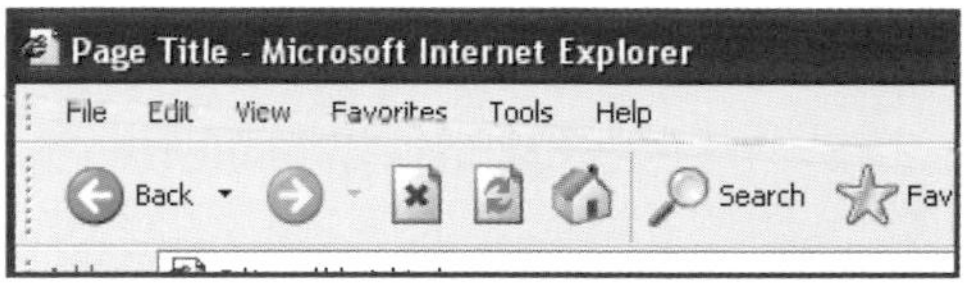

Figure 5.13 An untitled page.

▶ **Page name.** Like the title, the name of the page (the last part of the page's Web address) should be descriptive. For example, use `about-weight-loss.html` instead of something generic like `page2.html`. (The page name is also used by AdSense.) Page names should consist of numbers and lowercase letters only, although you can separate keywords with hyphens.

▶ **Headings.** Headings should also be descriptive. The main heading should match or be similar to the page title, though it can be longer. Be consistent with your capitalization.

▶ **Summary.** For long pages, the first sentence or paragraph of body text on the page (that is, text that is not a heading) should summarize the rest of the page so the reader knows at a glance what the page is about.

▶ **Locator.** A locator shows the path to a page (**Figure 5.14**). It's often just a single line of links separated by arrow characters (>). Locators are useful when pages are grouped together in sections: Visitors can quickly move to other pages in the path by clicking on parts of the locator. (Some sites like to include path information in the title as well, as in "About Diabetes — Articles," but this doesn't replace the locator.)

Keywords

Since they're also used by AdSense to determine the page's topic, include keywords in headings whenever possible.

First Sentence Is Key

The first sentence of a page is especially important, as it is used by search engines to describe the page unless you provide an alternate description.

Nav Bar Highlighting

If you use a navigation bar, be sure to highlight the appropriate part of the bar as an additional clue.

Books > Subjects > Children's Books > Ages 4-8

Figure 5.14 A locator shows the path to a page.

- **Site name.** Repeat the name of the Web site (dropping the initial `www`) on the page somewhere to reinforce your site's "brand," especially if you're using a name that reads better in mixed case. For example, `MakeEasyMoneyWithGoogle.com` instead of `www.makeeasymoneywithgoogle.com`, or `VoIP-at-home.com` instead of `www.voip-at-home.com`.

Showcasing Your Content

Claude looked up from his notepad (he'd been writing furiously as I talked) and whistled. "It all seems obvious when you describe it," he said, "but there sure are a lot of things about Web-site design that I hadn't thought of before."

"Trust me, Claude," I replied, "you can spend *hours* thinking about this stuff."

"I don't!" said Stef. "There's nothing for me to do—my blog already has a design."

"True," I agreed, "but there are still things for you to worry about. Most blog pages are generated using *templates*—pages with placeholders for content—that someone else designed. Several templates are usually available. Which template do you use? What color scheme works best? Where do you put the navigational aids like calendars and category lists? If your blog is just one part of a larger Web site, can you make it look like the rest of the site?"

Stef was disappointed. "I thought I had it easy!"

"You do," I said, "because the templates give you something to start with, a structure on which to design and build the blog.

Conventional Web sites don't have that—in effect, you start with a blank canvas."

"And as a painter," said Anita, whose hobby is watercolor painting, "I can assure you that a blank canvas can be pretty scary!"

"Can't you get templates for Web sites, too, not just blogs?" asked Claude.

"Yes, you can," I answered. "A few templates are often included with commercial Web-site editing software. You can also download templates—some for free, others for a small fee—from various Web sites. Or your hosting service may provide you with templates as part of a basic Web-site creation service."

"Or you can just do it all yourself," Anita said.

"That's the other choice, yes," I agreed. "It's not that hard once you learn some HTML, which I'll discuss at a later session. No template is perfect, either—they're really just starting points. But we're getting ahead of ourselves again, because so far all we've talked about is *site* design. We need to switch gears and talk about *page* design and how to showcase the site's content."

"And the ads!" Claude insisted, obviously concerned that I was forgetting the whole point of these sessions.

"And leaving plenty of room for ads," I agreed.

Page Layout

The basic structure of a page—the arrangement and positioning of its different parts—is referred to as its *layout*. While many layouts are possible, a standard layout for text-oriented pages is shown in **Figure 5.15**. The horizontal area at the top of the layout is the page *header* and the corresponding area at the bottom is the *footer*. Sandwiched between the header and the footer are one to three columns which we'll call *panes*.

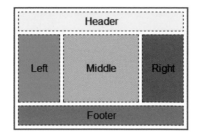

Figure 5.15
A standard layout for text-oriented pages.

A common configuration is the three-pane layout, with a navigation bar in the left pane, the page content in the middle pane, and ads in the right pane (**Figure 5.16**). Other configurations are also available. If the navigation bar is in the header, for example, you might use a two-pane format, with content on one side and ads on the other. Or you might use a single-pane format and place the ads in the header and/or the footer. Or insert them in the middle of the content—there are AdSense formats for every possible situation!

Figure 5.16 A typical page, with a navigation bar on the left, content in the middle, and ads on the right.

If you can't decide what page layout to use, model your site after a favorite Web site. Sketch it out on paper and see if you like it. Whatever you do, though, *be consistent* and use the same layout throughout the site wherever you can.

Design Principles

Entire books have been written on how (and how *not*) to design Web pages. Unless you're a graphic designer by training, your pages won't be works of art filled with special effects. Your goal is to create attractive pages that are easy to read. Do it by following simple design principles:

▸ **Add white space.** The term *white space* refers to the empty areas surrounding blocks of text and other page elements. Leaving out white space is a common mistake. Compare the crowded text block in **Figure 5.17** to the same block in **Figure 5.18**. Notice how the white space makes the text much more attractive and readable.

> This is an example of some text crowded into a box. Notice how hard it is to read the text because it's right up against the borders of the box. It's important to use *whitespace* to make it more readable.

Figure 5.17 A lack of white space makes the text harder to read.

> This is an example of some text with some whitespace around it. Notice how easier it is to read the text because of the additional whitespace.

Figure 5.18 White space makes the text block much more readable.

▸ **Choose one or two standard fonts.** There are probably several dozen *fonts* (typefaces) installed on your computer, but have you ever used more than two or three of them?

Copyright Issues

The *design* of a Web page is also protected by copyright, just like the content. If you duplicate someone else's site down to the last detail, you can be sued for copyright violation. That's why other sites should be used as models only.

Using Templates

When you base your design on a template, make sure you understand the conditions attached to the template—the template may require attribution and a link back to the site it came from.

White Space

Good page designs incorporate plenty of white space.

Using multiple fonts on the same page is a definite no-no because it makes the text harder to read. (The one exception is headings, which are sometimes in a font different from that of the body text.) The same goes for special effects like blinking text—avoid them like the plague. We'll talk more about fonts in the next chapter.

▶ **Use a white or light background.** Dark text on a light-colored background (white, ideally) is much easier to read due to the high contrast between the two colors. This is why most printed documents are done in black ink on bright white paper. **Figures 5.19** and **5.20** show the difference in readability between high-contrast and low-contrast colors.

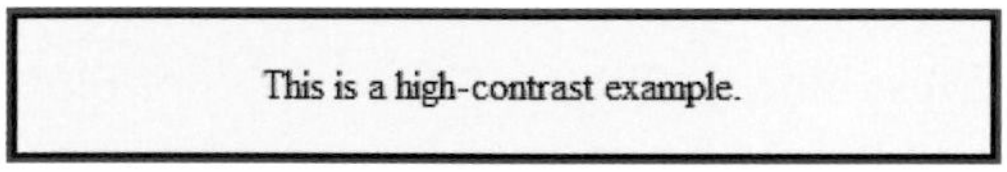

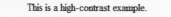

Figure 5.19 A high-contrast example.

Figure 5.20 A low-contrast example.

▶ **Don't be afraid of color, but use it sparingly.** On the other hand, you don't want your pages to be black and white only. Color can be used to highlight or emphasize text for added visual impact. Browsers already use color to distinguish visited links from unvisited links. You can use color to emphasize headings or to shade table backgrounds for easier reading. It's also common to change the background color for headers and footers and the parts of the page layout that are outside the panes.

Colors on the Web

When the Web was in its infancy, many computer systems could display only 256 colors on screen. Unfortunately, the different operating systems used slightly different *color palettes* (color sets), which created variations in graphics and images that should have looked identical. To combat this, a "Web-safe" or "browser-safe" color palette was developed that could be used consistently across all systems. Now that the vast majority of systems can display many more colors, though, the need for the browser-safe palette has all but disappeared.

Web-Safe Colors

Details of the Web-safe color palette scheme are well documented by author and graphic designer Lynda Weinman at www.lynda.com/hex.html.

Above the Fold

Place the interesting or important material at the top of the page to ensure that the visitor sees it—if it's near the bottom, they'll only see it if they scroll down the page.

▶ **Keep pages short and not too wide.** Don't cram reams of text onto a single page and overwhelm the reader. Spreading the text across several pages also exposes the reader to more ads, which can only benefit you. Make sure your text blocks aren't too wide—shorter columns are easier to read.

▶ **Be printer-friendly.** Speaking of wide pages, there's nothing more frustrating than printing a Web page and ending up with cut-off text. Ensure that your pages print properly, or else provide alternate "printer-friendly" versions that do.

▶ **Keep the interesting or important material "above the fold."** In the newspaper industry, the term "above the fold" refers to the top part of a folded newspaper page, the first part that a reader sees. In Web design, the term refers to the part of a Web page that is initially visible in a normal-sized browser window (**Figure 5.21**).

Alt Browsers

Find out more about Firefox at www.mozilla.org/products/firefox/. Apple's Safari browser, which works only on Mac OS X, can be downloaded at www.apple.com/safari/.

Keep Ads Separate

The AdSense terms of service require you to place the ads on your page in such a way that visitors don't confuse them with the page content.

Figure 5.21 Keep the important material "above the fold" so the visitor always sees it.

▸ **Support different browsers.** Some people don't use Microsoft's Internet Explorer as their Web browser, though many site designers apparently assume that everyone does. Alternative browsers like Firefox and Apple's Safari are just as important, so you should ensure that your site looks good and behaves properly with as many browsers as possible. (Text-based sites and blogs are less likely to have problems than graphic-intensive or dynamically generated sites, but it's always good to check.)

▸ **Group and separate page elements.** Clear boundaries between the different parts of a page make it obvious what's what. You can use white space to do this, or you can use graphic cues like lines and boxes.

You can find other design tips on the Web. Two Web sites in particular stand out. The first is the Web Style Guide, `www.webstyleguide.com`, a free online guide to Web-site design. The second is Web Pages That Suck, `www.webpagesthatsuck.com`, a site that showcases examples of *bad* design so that you can learn what *not* to do.

Too Much Thinking

"I never realized that there was so much *thinking* required to set up a Web site," Claude said. "Is it always like this?"

"No," I replied, "because the first site is always the hardest. You're learning a lot of new concepts. The second and third sites are always easier—especially if you're reusing the same design."

"Second and third sites?" Anita asked. "You expect us to build more than *one* site?"

"Well, no," I said, shaking my head. "I don't *expect* you to, but I won't be surprised if you do. Once your site is up and running and you have some spare time again, you may be tempted to start another site."

Claude nodded. "Financial advisors are always talking about having multiple streams of income—same thing, I guess."

"That's assuming you're making significant money from the sites, yes," I agreed, "but nobody can guarantee that. But let's not count our chicks before they've hatched. I think we're done talking about design, so I want you to go home now and think about how you want your site to look. We'll meet together again to learn how to build Web pages, and then I'll spend time with each of you to get you started with your site."

"I'm just a blogger…Do I really need to learn how to build Web pages?" Stef asked.

"Remember," I explained, "your blog is fundamentally a set of Web pages. If you want to modify your blog's template, for example, you'll need to understand how to build a Web page. Besides, you may decide to set up your own Web site at some point—you might as well learn about it now!"

We set another meeting time—at my house again—and parted ways. Claude seemed pretty excited, so I reminded him to stay away from the blinking text. He would, he promised, and they all laughed as they walked out the door.

chapter six

Building Your Site

> Anita: Today we're going to learn about HTML. Isn't that programming?

> Eric: HTML isn't a programming language, it's a markup language. The term comes from the publishing industry, where instructions for things like fonts, spacing, and margins were added to book manuscripts to tell the printers what to do.

> Anita: Wouldn't you do that with a word processor?

> Eric: Exactly! Except that Word's hiding the markup from you.

> Anita: So can I use Word to create my Web pages?

> Eric: You can because Word has an option to save a document as HTML. But I wouldn't recommend it, because the HTML it creates isn't that great. You're better off using proper Web-page editing software.

HTML

HTML is an abbreviation for HyperText Markup Language. *Hypertext* is the original term for electronic documents connected by instantaneous links. For more on the first hypertext project, see http://xanadu.com/

When the three returned to my house for our next session, I could tell that Anita was a bit wary. Stef and Claude seemed eager, however, so I asked Anita what was wrong.

"Well," Anita began, "I'm wondering how technical this session's going to be. Dad may like this stuff, but I don't think either of us"—she glanced over at Stef—"finds it very interesting."

"Actually," Stef said, "I'm more interested than you think. I didn't like the way my blog looked, so I got my friend to show me enough so I could change it. It was easier than I thought it'd be."

As I motioned for the three of them to sit down, I tried to allay Anita's fears. "Well, Stef, you're ahead of the other two, but it won't take them long to catch up," I said. "I promised you at the beginning that there would be no programming involved, and I'm not changing that promise. You can build a Web site without doing any coding."

Anita spoke up. "But today we're going to learn about HTML. Isn't that programming?"

"A fair question," I answered, "but the answer is no. HTML isn't a programming language, it's a *markup language*—that's what the ML in HTML stands for, in fact."

"Still sounds geeky to me," Anita said with a grimace.

"It's not that geeky," I assured her. "The term comes from the publishing industry, where instructions were added to the margins of book manuscripts to tell the printers what to do. This was called *marking up* the document."

"What kind of instructions?" Claude asked.

"Fonts, spacing, margins—the things that affect the look of a book," I explained.

"Wouldn't you do that with a word processor?" Anita said.

"Exactly!" I said, glad she had made the connection. "Publishers usually don't mark up paper documents anymore; they use word processors, document formatters, and other software tools. Instead of being on paper, the markup is stored electronically in the document files along with the actual document."

"So when I use Word, I'm using a markup language?" Stef asked.

"Yes," I said, "except that Word's hiding the markup from you. But when you bold a word in a paragraph, for example, Word inserts markup around the text you bolded. When Word goes to display or print the text, it sees the markup and turns on bolding until more markup turns the bolding off."

"And styles are markup too?" she asked, referring to Word's name for collections of formatting instructions.

"Uh-huh," I nodded, "they're just sequences of markup instructions labeled with descriptive names like Heading 1 or Bullet List. You can do similar things with Web pages, too."

"My friend showed me some of that when we customized my blog," Stef said, "but I don't have to worry *too* much about this stuff because there's a Web page on my blog that lets me add new entries. It lets me do bolding, links, and images, so I guess it adds all the markup automatically." I nodded agreement.

"Well," Anita said, "I don't have a blog…so can I use Word to create my Web pages? I know how to use Word."

"You can," I admitted, "because Word has an option to save a document as HTML. But I wouldn't recommend it, because the HTML it creates isn't that great. You're better off using proper Web-page editing software."

"What software do you recommend?" Claude asked.

"Funny you asked," I said, "because I spent some time the other day looking at what's currently available in preparation for this meeting.

Get Nvu

The Nvu open-source page layout application is available at www.nvu.com.

I was looking for something free that was simple enough for nonexperts to use. The best one I found is an application called *Nvu*. There's even a version of it for the Mac, Stef, in case you want to do more than just blog. Let's take a look at it and see how easy it is to build Web pages."

Creating Web Pages with Nvu

"Is Nvu free the way Firefox is free?" Stef asked.

"Yes," I said, "it's what us techies call *open source* software, which means that it's developed and supported by a community of programmers, not just a single company. Here's what the Nvu Web site says about the software."

> *Nvu (pronounced N-view, for a "new view") makes managing a web site a snap. Now anyone can create web pages and manage a web site with no technical expertise or knowledge of HTML.*

"Sounds perfect!" Claude said.

"It's actually quite good," I agreed, "and the price is certainly perfect for our needs. When you get home, I want you all to go to the Nvu Web site and download the latest version of Nvu. Now, let me start the editor and show you what I mean. And Claude, you're going to be my guinea pig. Did you bring me the information I requested?"

"Yeah," he said, "I signed up for hosting and I printed out the email they sent me."

"Great," I said, "because we're going to build some pages and place them on your VoIP-at-Home.com site. You're about to create a Web presence! So let's get cracking."

Getting Started with Nvu

Launch Nvu for the first time and you'll see a window like the one shown in **Figure 6.1**. At the top are toolbars similar to a word processor's. On the left side is the Nvu Site Manager, and on the right is the page editor. The page editor is where you create and edit the page.

Making Room

If you need extra room when working with Nvu, close the site manager—you can reopen it when needed.

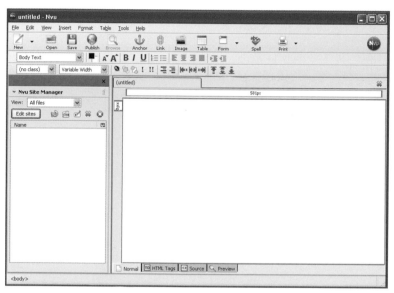

Figure 6.1 The Nvu application window.

Before proceeding, select Preferences from the Tools menu to bring up the Nvu Options dialog. Uncheck the checkbox labeled "Use CSS styles instead of HTML elements and attributes." This will simplify the HTML that the editor creates. We'll discuss what CSS is later, when we talk about styles.

Nvu automatically creates a blank Web page for you when it starts. Before going any further, select Page Title and Properties from the Format menu to display the Page Properties dialog (**Figure 6.2**).

You can set basic information about the Web page from this dialog, including:

▶ The title displayed in the browser's title bar when the page is viewed

▶ The page's author

▶ A short description of the page

▶ The language in which the page is written

Figure 6.2 The Page Properties dialog.

Every page needs a title. In this case, it's "VoIP-at-Home.com: Internet Telephoning at Home" because we're building the home page for Claude's site. Nvu will refuse to save the page until you set its title, so you might as well do it first. Most of the other properties can be left as is except for the description and the language. The page description is shown by Google and other search engines on its search-results page, so take the time to write a short phrase that describes what the page (and the site) is about and that will attract searchers to your site. The language should be set to "en" (short for "English") unless you're writing your page in a different language.

Now save the page by selecting Save As from the File menu—it's always a good idea to save the page as soon as you set its title. Create a folder for the site and save the page there. Nvu will suggest a name for you based on the title, but remember to follow the page title rules from Chapter 5 and use lowercase letters and no spaces. Since we're creating the home page for Claude's site, the File name should be the standard "index.html."

You're ready to add content to the *body*, the part of the page that is shown by the browser when it loads the page. The body is currently empty, but the page itself isn't empty: The information you entered in the Page Properties dialog is stored in the *head* of the page, which isn't shown by the browser. To see the head, switch Nvu to the Source view, either by selecting HTML Source from the View menu or by clicking the Source tab at the bottom of the window (**Figure 6.3**). The source view shows the raw HTML that Nvu stores when you save the file. You don't need to use this, so switch back to the Normal view by clicking the Normal tab. The Normal view is where you do most of your work.

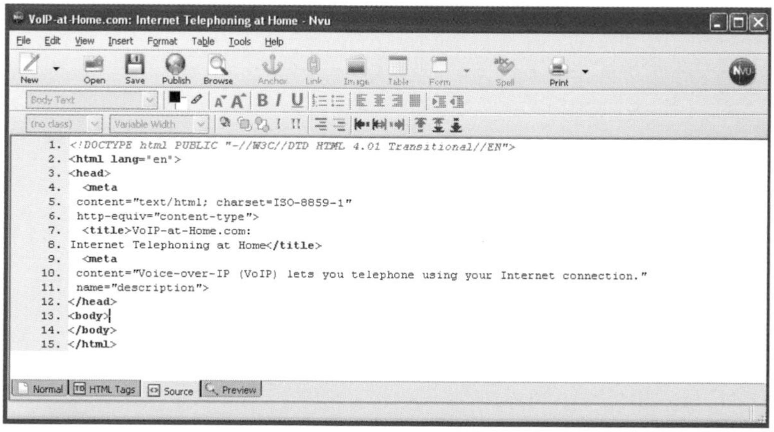

Your Preference

Note that default values for most of Nvu's properties can be set from the Nvu Options dialog.

Title Chop-Chop

If a title is too long to fit in the title bar, the browser will truncate it (cut the last part off) to make it fit. Make sure the title is readable if it's shortened.

Figure 6.3 The Nvu Source view.

A Web page is built out of *page elements* and *styles*. Page elements describe the structure of the page: This is a heading, this is a paragraph, this is a link to another page, and so on. Page elements are edited in the Normal view, which looks and behaves a lot like a word processor. Styles establish how the page elements are to be displayed: Bold the headings, use an eleven-point font for paragraphs, color links blue, and so on. In other words, page elements are like nouns (things) and styles are like verbs (actions). Styles are edited in a separate view, which we'll discuss later.

To create new page elements, type directly into the Normal view as you would with a word processor. For Claude's home page, I entered a heading, a subheading, an introductory paragraph, and a copyright line (**Figure 6.4**).

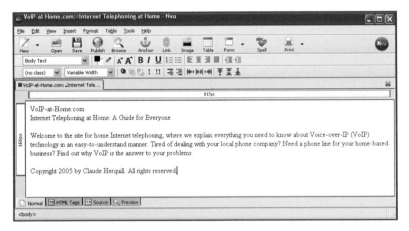

Figure 6.4 The initial text for Claude's home page.

By default, each paragraph you enter is created as a page element called *Body Text*. You can change a paragraph from one type of element to another by first selecting it with the mouse and then choosing an option from the Paragraph submenu of the Format menu (**Figure 6.5**). For the heading, select the *Heading 1* page element. The subheading should be changed to *Heading 2*. Change the two remaining paragraphs to the *Paragraph* type. The page now looks different: The headings are in larger, bolded fonts and the paragraphs are farther apart than they were before (**Figure 6.6**).

Quicker Page Elements

To make page element changes more quickly, use the leftmost drop-down list in the toolbar.

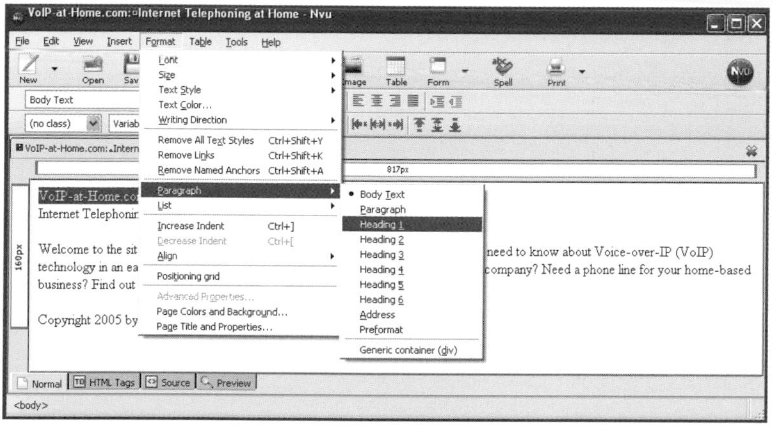

Figure 6.5 Changing the type of a paragraph.

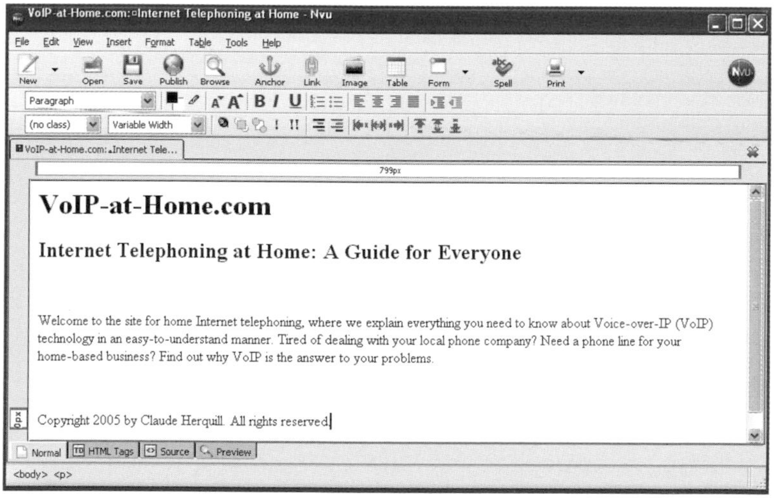

Figure 6.6 Claude's home page with the new page elements.

Text within a paragraph can also be formatted, just as with a word processor, by using the toolbar icons to bold and italicize text or even change its size. Don't forget to save the page after changing it.

Peeking Under the Hood

Since we were working on his site, Claude was extremely interested in what I was doing. He wanted more details, though. "Can I see the Source view again?" Claude asked.

"Sure," I said, "in fact, why don't you take control. This is your site we're building, after all." I moved my chair over so Claude could sit in front of the computer. Once he was settled, he switched Nvu back to the Source view to see the raw HTML that the editor had generated (**Figure 6.7**).

"Very interesting," he said. "This is actually pretty readable. Those words in angle brackets are the page elements, right?"

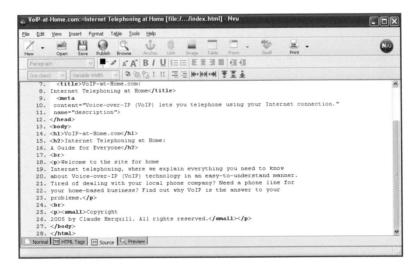

Figure 6.7 Viewing the raw HTML in the Source view.

"Right," I said. "They're called *tags*. They usually come in pairs—one to start a markup command, one to end it."

"And the end one has a slash in it?" Claude asked.

"Yep."

"The spacing doesn't matter much, does it?" Stef noticed.

"No," I agreed, "you can pretty much put as many spaces and carriage returns as you want between most things. The browser doesn't care, but it's definitely easier for us to read if there's lots of white space."

"So what's this view all about, then?" Claude asked as he clicked the HTML Tags tab between the Normal and Source tabs. "Hmmm…it's like the Normal view, but it shows you where the tags start." He clicked the H2 tag and the subheading was selected (**Figure 6.8**).

"It makes it easy to select the text that the tag applies to!" Stef said.

Learning HTML

The W3Schools site www.w3schools.com/html offers a very thorough tutorial on HTML. For a quick list of common HTML tags, see www.w3schools.com/html/html_quick.asp.

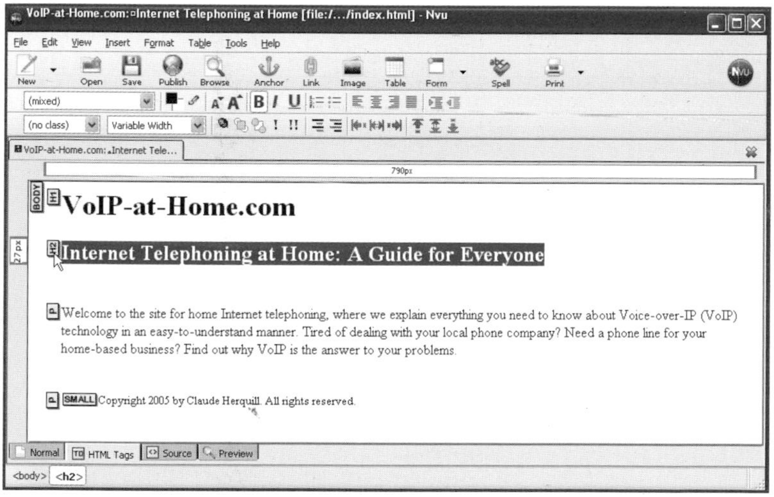

Figure 6.8 The HTML Tags view.

"Can I change the page from this view, too?" Claude wondered. I nodded yes. "OK, I want to add a copyright symbol to the last line." He started looking through the menus. "Let me see, Word lets you insert symbols from a menu. I wonder if this program does….Ah! There it is, under Insert!" He selected Characters and Symbols from the menu, and a dialog popped up. He found the copyright symbol in the drop-down list, clicked the Insert button, and dismissed the dialog.

"This *is* pretty easy," he said as he clicked the Preview tab next to the Source tab. "Funny, this view looks just like the Normal view—I thought it'd be different."

"That's because you're not doing anything complicated in the Normal view," I explained. "If you do, the Preview will show you what it *should* look like in a browser."

"Should?" Anita asked. "Can it be different?"

"Well," I replied, "browsers have different behaviors, yes, so if you're doing complicated layouts, you should definitely see how the page looks in different browsers. There's a Browse icon on the toolbar that displays the page in the Web browser you normally use. But for simple layouts, the built-in Preview should be fine."

Claude switched back to the Normal view. "Can we jazz this page up? It's not very exciting! And there are no links anywhere."

"We'll get to that, but not just yet," I said. "First, let's publish the page to your Web site."

Publishing the Page

"All right, Claude, you stay at the keyboard," I continued, "and let's see if you can figure out what to do."

Claude scanned the Nvu menus and toolbar. "Well," he said, "there's a big button here labeled 'Publish,' so I'm going to click it." He did, and the Publish Page dialog appeared (**Figure 6.9**). "Huh. OK, what now?" asked Claude.

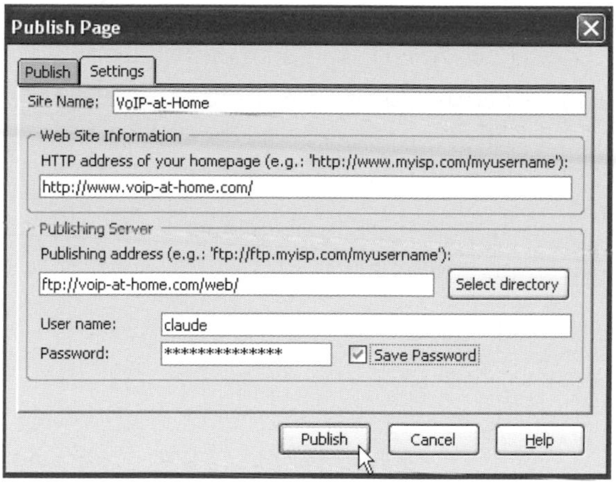

Figure 6.9 The Publish Page dialog.

"Before you can place the HTML file on your Web site, you need to create what Nvu calls a *publishing site*," I explained. "The publishing site tells Nvu how to connect to the hosting service's computer. The information you need is in the email the hosting service sent you." Claude reached for the printout he'd brought. "Nvu supports multiple publishing sites, so you give them names to tell them apart."

"All right," Claude said, "we'll call the site 'VoIP-at-home,' but I'll drop the `.com` part. The HTTP address of the homepage is `http://www.voip-at-home.com`. The publishing address…hmm…the mail from the hosting service says that I should FTP to `voip-at-home.com/web`. What's FTP?"

Stef jumped in at that point. "I know! It stands for *file transfer protocol*," she said. "It's for copying files from one computer to another."

"Right," I said. "So type in '`ftp://voip-at-home.com/web`' as the publishing address, and then enter the user ID and password that they sent you."

"Dad's FTP address is a lot different than the one my hosting service sent me," Stef said.

"They're not as standard as Web addresses," I explained, "but it shouldn't matter as long as you use the address they supplied you. Now, Claude, you're ready to publish."

Claude hit the Publish button. Another dialog appeared as Nvu copied the index.html file from my computer to Claude's hosting service (**Figure 6.10**).

Figure 6.10 Publishing the page to the hosting service.

"It's done," Claude said, "so can I try my Web page now?" I nodded, and Claude opened a browser window and typed the address of his site, `www.voip-at-home.com`. "There it is!" he yelled as the home page appeared (**Figure 6.11**).

"Yay Dad!" Stef said, and Anita was smiling, too.

"Great job, Claude," I said. "Now let's add another page to your site and link it to your home page. Anita, will you please take the helm?" I motioned her over and Claude switched seats with her. "I know this is your father's site, but I want each of you to try editing a Web page. All right, we need to create an about page and link it to the home page and vice versa. Why don't you go ahead and show me how to do it?"

Figure 6.11 The Web page is now live on the site.

Adding and Linking Pages

Adding a page with Nvu is as easy as clicking the New icon on the toolbar, setting its title, and saving it to disk. Anita was able to figure this out in short order. She titled the new page "About VoIP-at-Home.com" and saved it to disk as "about.html." She added a heading and a couple of paragraphs. The home page was still accessible from within Nvu, so she quickly copied the copyright line from the home page to finish the simple about page (**Figure 6.12**).

Now it was time to link the two pages. Anita moved the cursor to the top of the about page and inserted a blank paragraph. Then she clicked the Link button to open the Link Properties dialog (**Figure 6.13**). After entering "Home" for the link text and "index.html" for the link location, she clicked the OK button to create the new link. Pleased with herself, she immediately went to the bottom of the page and highlighted her father's name in the copyright message, then clicked the Link button again. She had noticed the email address option on the Link Properties dialog. She checked the option and entered her father's email address, `claude@voip-at-home.com`, to create a second link on the about page (**Figure 6.14**). Clicking this link would send an email to Claude.

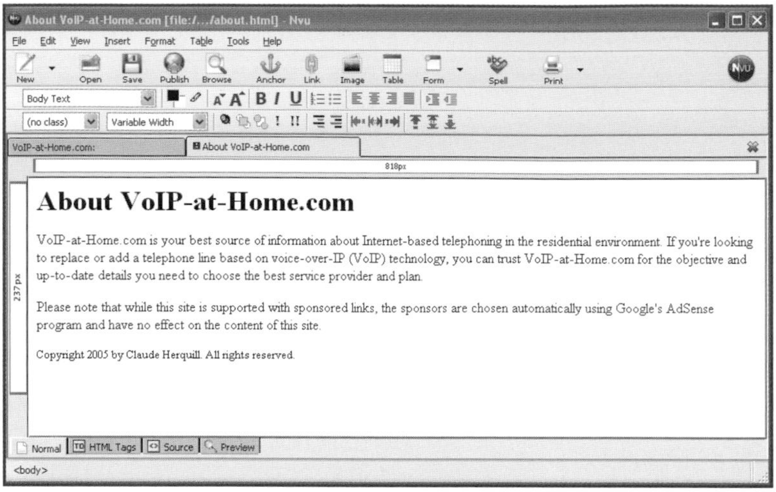

Figure 6.12 The newly created about page.

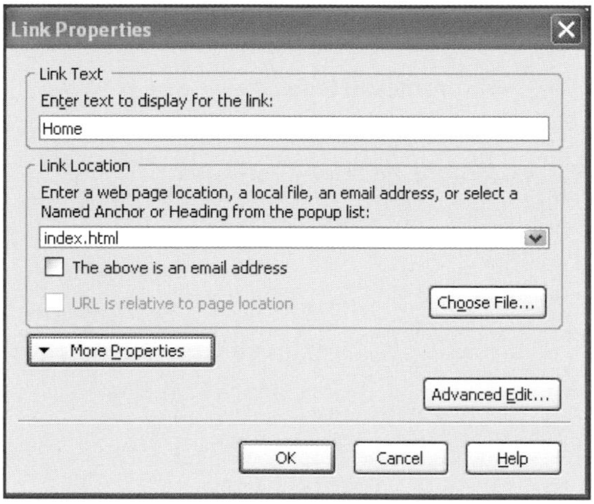

Figure 6.13 The Link Properties dialog.

Feeling very confident, Anita then switched to the home page and added a link to it, a link called "About this site" that referenced the about.html page. She also added an email link. When she was done, she clicked the Publish button to update the site.

section three | Design

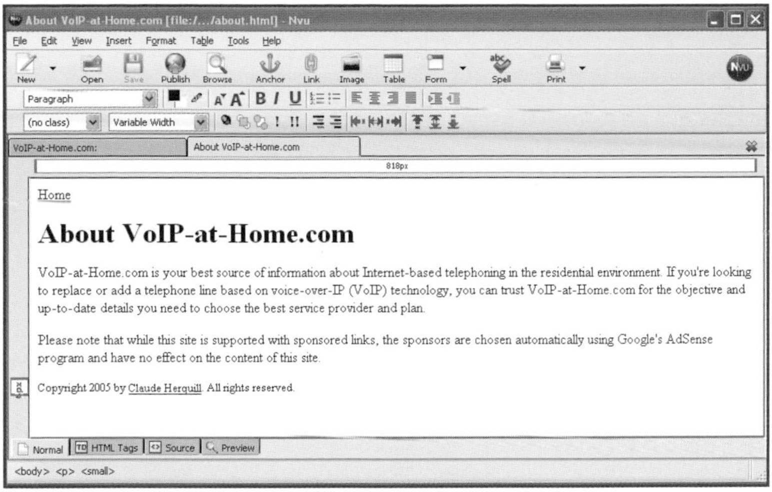

Figure 6.14 The about page with its new links.

Testing and More Testing

"Look," Anita said, "here's the updated home page." She activated the browser window and reloaded the page, which now sported two links. "And here's the new about page," she continued, clicking the "About this site" link. Unfortunately, the page didn't show up because the browser couldn't find it.

"You forgot to publish the about page," I explained to her. "What you've got now on the home page is called a *broken link*, because the page it links to is missing. Don't worry, it's a common mistake—even professionals do it. That's why you should always check your changes *before* you publish a page. Check it visually in the Preview view, then use the Browse button to load it into a browser and check the links."

"Like I always proofread my reports before submitting them," Stef said, as Anita clicked the Browse button to check the about page.

"What does this mean?" she asked, pointing to a new dialog on the screen (**Figure 6.15**).

Figure 6.15 Asking for permission to launch a browser window.

"It's a bit cryptic," I agreed. "Nvu's asking your permission to launch a browser. Click the Launch Application button to continue."

As soon as she did, a new browser window displaying the about page appeared. She clicked the Home link to load the home page. She then clicked "About this site" again to return to the about page. She also tested the email links at the bottom of each page.

"Everything looks good," she said, "so let me publish the about page." She did, and this time when she clicked the "About this site" link on the `www.voip-at-home.com` home page, the about page was loaded.

"Perfect!" I said. "Two pages up already. Now let's beautify them a bit."

Making Good-Looking Pages

"Hey, I know what to do," Claude said, taking back control from Anita. "You just use the toolbar buttons to change fonts and colors, just like in a word processor." Claude showed us what he meant by selecting a heading and clicking buttons on the toolbar to make the text larger and center it on the page.

"You're right, Claude," I said, "that's the simplest way to do things. But it's not the best way."

"Why not?" he wondered.

"Because you're not letting the browser do the work for you," I explained. "Why change the font size and color for each and every heading? The browser *knows* it's a heading, so tell the browser how you want the headings displayed and let *it* worry about the details."

"Huh," he said, "I guess that makes sense. Makes it easier to change your mind, too, right?"

"Exactly!" I answered, glad he understood it. "You tell the browser *once* how to display all the page elements used by your site. If you don't like something, you just change it in one place—there's no need to edit every single page."

"Those are the styles you mentioned before," Stef said. "Like Word's styles."

"Very much like those," I agreed, "except that Word styles define structure *and* presentation rules. In a Web page, the two concepts are separate: The page elements—the tags—define the structure, and the styles define how to present that structure. Let me show you what I mean."

Defining Your Own Styles

"As you might already guess," I said as I took control of the computer again, "your browser comes with a set of predefined styles for displaying page elements. You can usually change these styles to suit your own needs, such as making the default fonts larger or using different colors for links. As a Web page designer, however, you can define new styles to control how *your* pages look in the browser. In most cases, your styles take precedence."

"But visitors can always force the browser to use their preferences, right?" Anita asked.

CSS Ideas

The site http://cssvault.com/ showcases many Web sites that make creative use of cascading style sheets. It's a good place to check for design ideas.

"Right," I said. "You're not in *total* control. If visitors can't read your site because the fonts are too small, they're not going to care how much work you put into the design. They'll make the text bigger so they can read it. That's only fair. But only a very small percentage of your visitors will do that. Most will use the styles you define and see the site the way you meant it to be seen."

"Hey!" Stef said, "can you use the styles to control how a page is *printed*?"

"Yes, you can," I answered. "Why do you ask?"

"Because sometimes when I print a Web page it doesn't look at all like what it does on the screen," she explained.

"That's the other advantage to using styles," I said. "You can define different rules for displaying the page versus printing the page." Turning to the monitor, I opened Nvu's Tools menu and selected the CSS Editor menu item. "Since styles are different from page elements, you use a different editor to create them. This editor is called a *CSS editor*. CSS stands for *cascading style sheets*, which is the geek term for a set of Web-page styles." There was a new window on the screen titled "CSS Stylesheets" (**Figure 6.16**). "This editor makes it all pretty simple, so don't get caught up with the terminology."

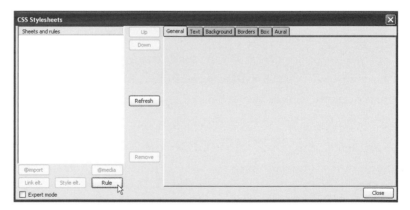

Figure 6.16 Nvu's style editor.

"The first thing you want to do," I continued, "is uncheck the Expert Mode checkbox at the bottom left-hand corner...there. Now you click the Rule button to create a new style rule." I did, and the editor prompted me for some details about the rule (**Figure 6.17**). "Let's change the way headings are displayed by creating a style that applies to all the Heading 1 page elements. You need the tag name for this, which you can get from either the HTML Tags view or the Source view of the HTML page. The tag for Heading 1 is 'h1.' Now I click the Create Style rule button to create an empty rule for h1 tags. OK, Claude, why don't you take over from here?" I shifted seats with Claude.

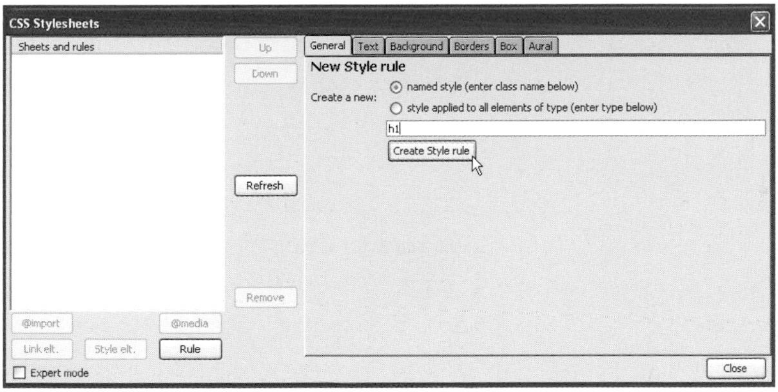

Figure 6.17 Creating a new style rule.

"What do I do now?" he asked.

"Look through the tabs on the right-hand side and change some of the properties," I answered.

"OK," he said as he clicked the Text tab, "I want the heading to be a nice green. Can I type the name of a color here?" Claude pointed to the input field labeled "Color."

"Try it," I said.

Safe Colors

Not all colors look the same in every browser. For an explanation of "browser-safe colors," examples of color charts, and more info on Web color, see www.websitetips.com/color/.

Claude typed "green" into the field. "Hey! It worked! Look at the heading!" He moved the editor window aside so we could see that the heading had indeed changed to green.

"Click the button next to the color field," I suggested. He did, and a color picker popped up (**Figure 6.18**). "If you can't name the color you want, just pick it here to create a special code for it."

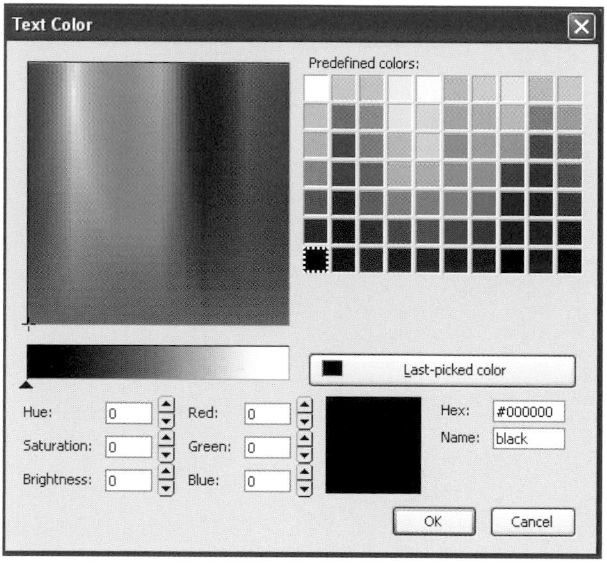

Figure 6.18 The color picker.

"I'm OK with just green for now," Claude said, dismissing the color picker. "But the typeface needs to be altered." Pausing, he looked closely at the options that were available. "What's a predefined font family? Is that what I want?"

"Probably," I answered. "A font family is a font or typeface name. Actually, it's a list of font names. Since not every font is available on all computers, you supply a list of fonts, and the visitor's browser goes through the list, looking for a match. The last name on the list is usually a generic one, like serif, sans-serif, or monospace, that the browser can always match to an existing font on the system." Claude was playing with the drop-down list of predefined font values as I said this (**Figure 6.19**).

Free Fonts

Need free fonts? There are many places on the Web to look. For starters, try www.fontfreak.com/ or www.fontfile.com/.

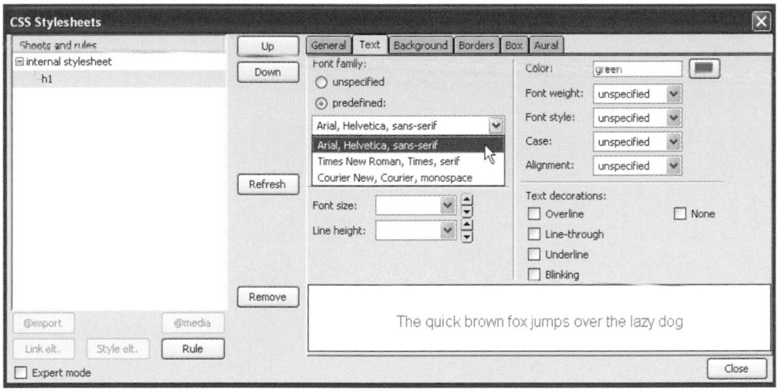

Figure 6.19 Setting text-related properties.

"All right," he said, "I'll choose one of the predefined values. Looks good. How do I put a line underneath it?" I told him there were two choices: He could underline just the words in the heading or else draw a line from one side of the browser window to the other. He wanted the latter, so he clicked the Borders tab and added a solid bottom border one pixel high. "Great! I think that's enough for the heading, but the subheading also needs to change. So I add a new rule for it, right?" I nodded. "All right…I'll add a rule for h2…change the font…set the color to black for variety…there!"

"You're almost done, I think," I said.

"I'd like a border around the whole page, though."

"OK, you need two rules for that," I said. "The first rule is for the body tag. Set the background color and the font." He set the color to light blue and the font to the same as the headings. "Now click the Rule button, but this time, instead of a page element style, you're going to add a *named style* called 'content.'" (see **Figure 6.20**).

"Now set its background color to white and then move to the Box page. This page is pretty complicated, but basically you're just here to set some margins. Set the margin values to 10px each—'px' is the abbreviation for pixel. Set the top and bottom padding values to 2px and the left and right padding to 10px. Then close the CSS editor."

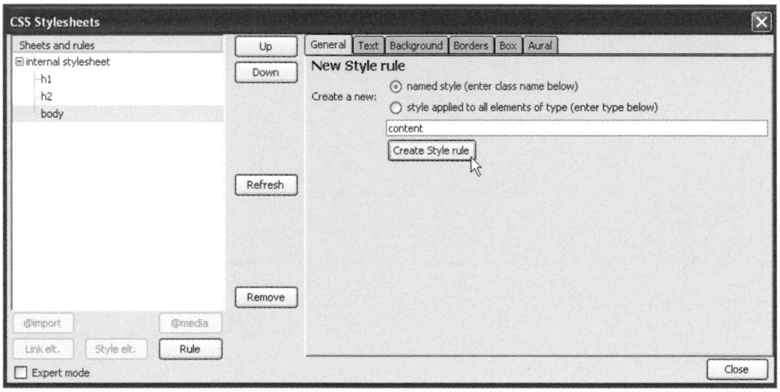

Figure 6.20 Creating a named style.

"Nothing's different," he said.

"First you have to add a couple of lines in the Source view," I said. "Here, let me show you." After switching to the Source view, I added a div tag—a division marker—at the start of the body and the matching end tag at the end of the body (**Figure 6.21**). Then I switched back to the Normal view.

"Hey!" Stef said. "That looks a lot better! What did you do?"

"A named style defines properties that you can apply to all different kinds of tags," I explained, "and the div tag basically just encloses whatever is inside it. By applying the content style to the div tag, we put a white box around and behind all the tags and text contained by the div tag. Now let's save and publish the page." After doing this, I reloaded the `www.voip-at-home.com` home page in a browser window (**Figure 6.22**).

"Looks like we're done!" said Claude.

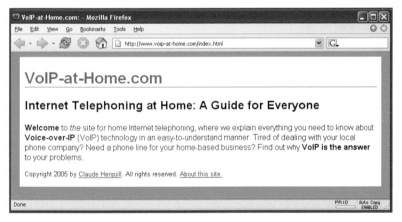

Figure 6.21 Adding a div tag to the page body.

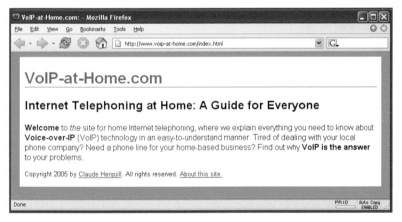

Figure 6.22 The new home page.

Sharing Styles across Pages

"Not quite," I said, shaking my head. "We've only fixed *one* page. The about page is still the same."

"So you need to copy the styles to it as well," Anita said.

"Yes, but there's an easier way to do it. Right now the styles we added to the home page are actually commands in the Web page. This is called an *embedded* or *internal* style sheet. We need to move them to a separate file, an *external* style sheet. Then multiple pages can link to it and share the style definitions."

"So the pages will all look the same," Stef concluded.

"Right," I agreed, "and if you want to change things across all pages, there's only one place to go." Turning back to the screen, I brought up the CSS editor again. "Luckily, Nvu makes it really easy to switch from an internal style sheet to an external style sheet. On the left-hand side of the window, click the internal stylesheet button, then click the button on the right-hand side called 'Export stylesheet and switch to exported version.'" The button was rather lengthy and hard to miss (**Figure 6.23**). "Nvu asks you for a file name, so enter '`styles.css`' or something similar, as long as it ends with `.css`—that's how the system knows it's a style sheet. And be sure to save the file in the same folder as your HTML pages."

"So now you're done?" Claude asked.

"Not yet," I answered, "because the style sheet isn't being referenced properly. Right now it's being loaded as a local file on your hard drive, which won't work after you publish it to the Web site. So we close the CSS editor again and switch to the Source view. Do you see the new link tag? You just need to change the href value in the tag to '`styles.css`' by itself." (See **Figure 6.24**.)

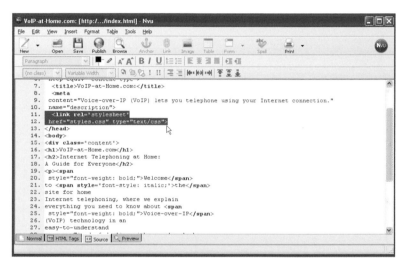

Figure 6.23 Switching to an external style sheet.

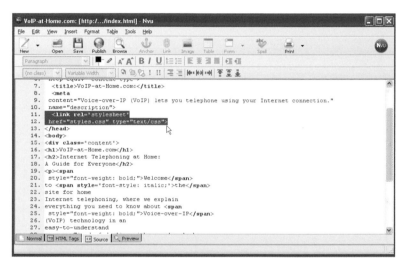

Figure 6.24 Changing the link tag.

"So do you just copy the link tag to the about page?" Stef asked.

"Yes," I said, "but don't forget to add the div tag there too." I made the changes to the about page and then saved both pages. "There.

Now we publish the pages. See how the style sheet is being copied up now?" (See **Figure 6.25**.)

Moving back to the browser window, I reloaded the about page at **www.voip-at-home.com/about.html** (**Figure 6.26**). "There," I said, "*now* we're done."

Figure 6.25 The style sheet is published with the page.

Figure 6.26 The style sheet applied to the about page.

Publishing a Blog

"I have a question," Stef said. "How do I publish my blog to my own Web site?"

"You're using Blogger, right?" I asked her. Blogger is Google's free blogging service. She nodded. "Then it's pretty easy. Here, take the keyboard and log into your Blogger account."

Stef went to `www.blogger.com` and logged in to her account (**Figure 6.27**).

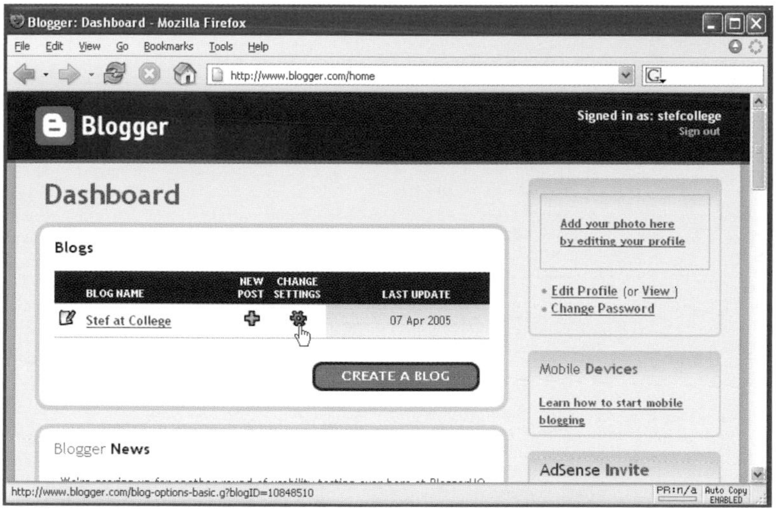

Get FTP

There are numerous standalone programs that let you access FTP sites and do file transfers. You can find links to many such utilities for Windows and Macintosh at http://compnetworking. about.com/cs/ novellgroupwise/.

Figure 6.27 Stef's Blogger dashboard.

"Change to your blog settings," I said, "and move to the Publishing section." (See **Figure 6.28**).

"I click the FTP link, then?" she asked. I nodded, and new settings were displayed (**Figure 6.29**).

Figure 6.28 Publishing settings for Stef's blog.

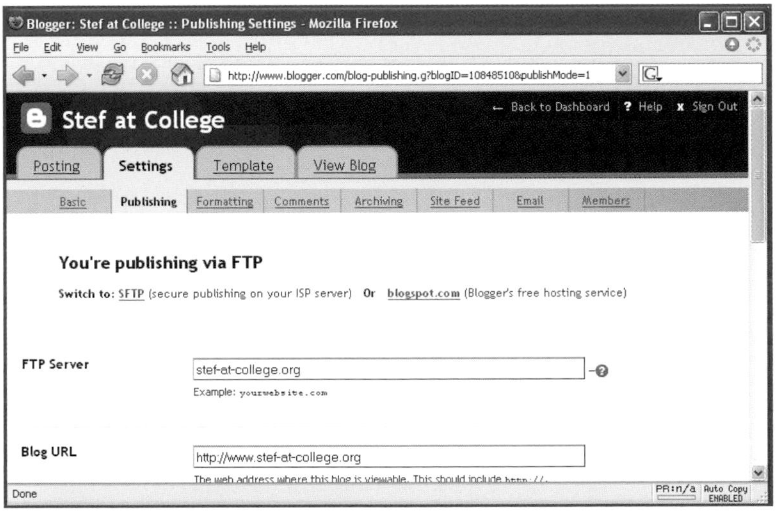

Figure 6.29 Setting the blog to publish via FTP to Stef's Web site.

section three | Design

"I see, I enter the FTP information here," she said. "So when I add an entry to my blog, it'll get copied over to my site?"

"Yep. That's it, you're done. And now," I said, checking my watch, "we're done, too."

Now the Real Work Starts

"That was a great session—I can't wait to get home and try this stuff out," said Claude.

"I'll mail you each the files so you have something to start with," I said. "But now the real work begins—you have to build some content."

"How soon can we apply for AdSense?" Anita asked.

"As soon as you have some decent content," I said. "Don't do it before then, though, there's no point. Get started on your sites—or work on your blog in your case, Stef—and send me regular updates. When you're ready to join, it's just a matter of filling out the form at www.google.com/adsense. It's easy. Then you wait a few days to see if you're accepted."

"What if we're not?" Claude wondered.

"We'll deal with that if it happens," I replied. "If you follow the rules we've already discussed, it shouldn't be a problem. So get to it, and we'll get together again once everyone's in the program." Unless I was mistaken, it would be at least a couple of weeks before we would meet again.

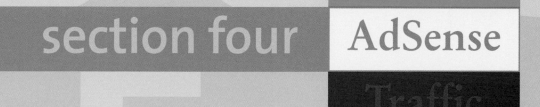

section four

Starting
Content
Design
AdSense
Traffic

chapter seven

Becoming an AdSense Publisher

> Stef: I've been showing ads since a couple of weeks ago. Blogger's online help pages show you how to add them to your blog's sidebar. So I did.

> Anita: So have you made any money?

> Stef: A bit. I've made over $10 so far. It's pretty exciting, actually—I check my AdSense account several times a day!

> Eric: You're doing great, and that's because you already had traffic coming to your site. But we'll save the traffic topic for later. Today we'll split our session into two parts. First, we're going to manage an AdSense account using the AdSense management console. In the second part, we'll use the console to publish ads on Web pages.

As it turned out, it was just over a month later when we all met again. This time we met at Claude's house, where his wife told me he'd been quite busy during the past few weeks. This I already knew, because he'd been asking me questions by email.

"I've been spending a lot of time working on my site," he said, waving to me as I entered.

"I know," I answered, "and I'm not surprised. Building a good site takes time. Did you have any problems joining AdSense?"

"No," Claude said. "I waited like you told us until I had at least a dozen good pages of content. The approval came by email within a couple of days."

"Great," I said, as I heard Claude's daughters greeting their mother at the door, "and it looks like the others are here now, too." Claude had moved his computer out to the dining room, so we sat down there and waited for the women to join us.

"Hey, guys!" Anita said. "Guess what? I got my AdSense approval yesterday."

"I got it three weeks ago," Stef said. "I applied as soon as I had moved my old blog entries over to the new blog."

"Good," I said, smiling, "it looks like we're all set. Have you all logged onto your AdSense accounts?" They all nodded.

"I'm already showing ads, you know," Stef said, seeming quite proud of herself.

"You are?" Claude asked. "Since when?"

"Since a couple of weeks ago," she explained. "Blogger's online help pages show you how to add them to your blog's sidebar. So I did."

"So have you made any money?" Anita asked.

"A bit. I've made over $10 so far," she said. "It's pretty exciting, actually—I check my AdSense account several times a day!"

"Some people check it hourly or even more frequently," I said. "It's fun to watch the pennies add up. You're doing great, and that's because you already had traffic coming to your site. Completely new sites won't make as much at the start—maybe not anything for the first while. They have to build their traffic first. But we'll save that topic for later. Today we'll split our session into two parts. First, we're going to manage an AdSense account using the AdSense management console. In the second part, we'll use the console to publish ads on Web pages."

Touring the AdSense Console

"Tell you what, Stef," I continued, "since you're an AdSense expert now, why don't you take over? You can demonstrate things with my AdSense account, if you want." She said that was fine, so I opened a browser window to **www.google.com/adsense** to access the AdSense login page (**Figure 7.1**).

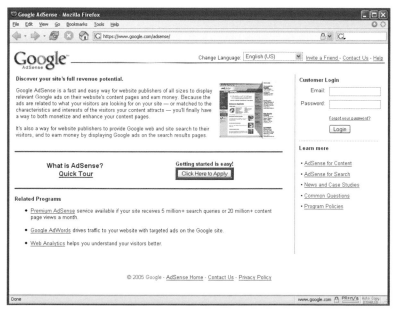

Figure 7.1 The AdSense login page.

Avoid Scams

Want the latest news on Internet scams and how to avoid them? Log on to www.scams.net/.

As I logged into my account, I gave them a warning. "Google uses a secure Web connection for AdSense account management, so if the Web address shown in your browser toolbar doesn't start with 'https:' and there's no lock icon in the browser status bar, don't log in—it's probably some kind of scam site looking to obtain your AdSense password."

"And always keep the password confidential," Claude added.

"Absolutely!" I said. "You don't want to let anyone access your account. Treat it like an online banking account. There, we're in. Your turn, Stef. Give us a tour."

Stef switched places with me. "OK," she began, "this is the AdSense management console. Right now it's showing the default page, the Ad Performance page." She pointed to the report displayed on the screen (**Figure 7.2**). "Normally, it shows you how much money you've earned today using AdSense."

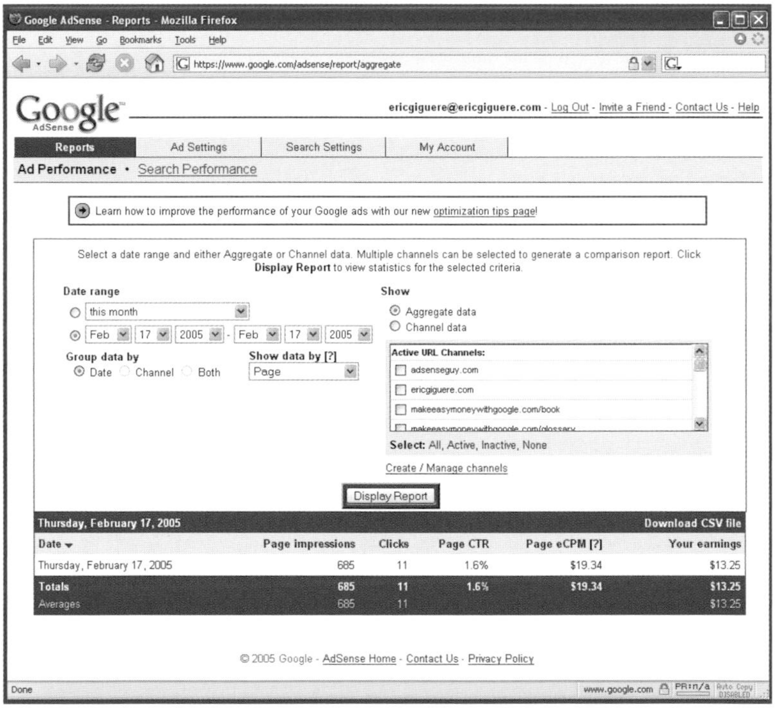

Figure 7.2 The Ad Performance page.

"That's what I really want to know!" Claude said.

"And it's updated throughout the day, as you pointed out," Stef continued, glancing at me. "But you can also generate reports for any range of dates. Of course, I only have a couple of weeks of data. How far back does it actually go?"

"To the day you displayed your first ad," I said. "In my case, that's August 8, 2003. Stef, do you see that message just above the report?"

"You mean the one in the box with the little arrow?" she said, pointing to it (**Figure 7.3**).

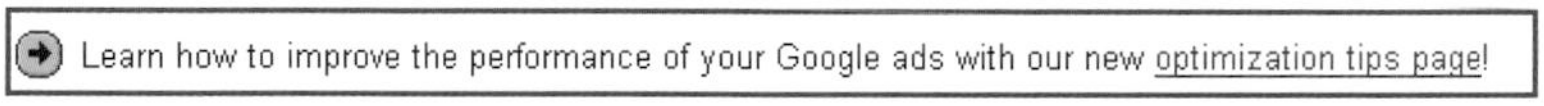

> ➔ Learn how to improve the performance of your Google ads with our new optimization tips page!

Figure 7.3 An AdSense announcement.

"That's how Google makes most of its announcements about AdSense," I explained, "so always be on the lookout for those. New features get added to AdSense all the time, so read them carefully. The management console was actually a lot simpler back when I first started with AdSense."

"Does Google ever send you email?" Anita asked.

"Sometimes," I replied, "for new feature announcements or when there's some kind of problem with your account or your Web sites. But I'll tell you about that later. Stef, please continue with the tour."

"Right," she said. "So at the top of the page are the tabs to switch between the major functions of the console." She clicked each tab in turn (**Figure 7.4**). "Reports to see how much you're earning. Ad Settings for creating ads, ad channels, and ad filters. Search Settings for creating search boxes, search channels, and search filters. My Account for managing your payment and tax information." Stef paused for a moment. "Huh. The My Account tab is different than it was last week, but I didn't actually notice it until just now."

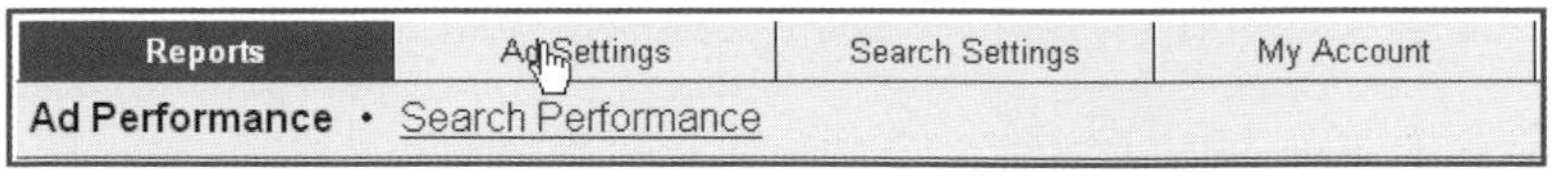

Figure 7.4 The management console tabs.

"I told you," I said, "AdSense is always changing. Sometimes it's subtle—they add another reporting option. Sometime's it's major—like when they added AdSense for search. You can usually tell when a major change occurs because Google updates the AdSense Terms and Conditions. When that happens, you're asked to agree to the new terms before Google lets you access your account."

"And if you don't agree?" Claude said.

"You're kicked out," I said, pretending to cut my throat with the side of my hand, "so you don't really have a choice but to agree if you want to stay in the program. But so far it's not been an issue— the Terms and Conditions have actually gotten more flexible as time's gone on. With Yahoo!'s entry into the game, I think you can expect even more features and flexibility."

"Where do I find the Terms and Conditions again?" Claude asked.

"I think there's a link to them in the online help," Stef answered, clicking the Help link at the top of the page and causing a new browser window to pop up (**Figure 7.5**). She scrolled the help page. "It's there at the bottom of the help page."

"Looks like there's a lot of help available," said Anita.

Stef agreed. "I've read through a lot of these items to help me understand AdSense."

"This is also where you can access the AdSense Preview Tool," I pointed out. "The Preview Tool lets you see what kind of ads AdSense would display on any random Web page."

Figure 7.5 The AdSense help page.

"But only with Internet Explorer on Windows, though," Stef said. "I couldn't use it on my Mac."

"But I have it installed, Stef," I said, "so why don't you open an Internet Explorer session and go to a random Web site. Now right-click the Web page and select the Google AdSense Preview Tool." A small window popped up. "You can click those ads if you want," I continued, "even if you're using the tool on your own site's pages, because the advertisers don't get charged for them."

"But why would you use this tool?" Anita asked.

"It lets you see what kind of ads will appear on new pages," I explained, "*before* you actually show ads on those pages. You see, it's a bad idea to add the code prematurely, before the page is finished, because AdSense may mistarget the ads. You can use the Preview Tool to see if the page is correctly targeted."

Stef was playing with the tool. "Or you can use it to see what kind of ads people in other countries see," she said, changing the tool to show us ads for Japanese visitors (**Figure 7.6**).

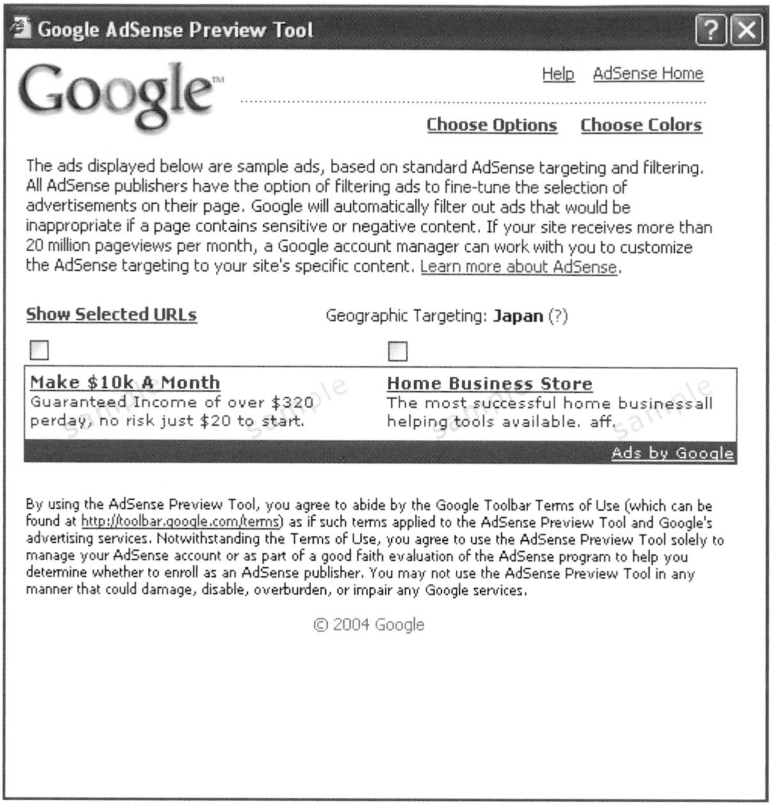

Figure 7.6 The AdSense Preview Tool.

"And that," I said, "concludes our initial tour of AdSense. Now we can—"

Claude interrupted me.

"What's that 'Invite a Friend' link at the top of the console?" he asked.

"It's for referring AdSense to your friends," I answered. "If you know anyone who has a Web site, you ask Google to send them an invitation to join the program."

"Do you get paid if they do?" Stef asked. "Friends of mine are always trying to get me to join things because they'll make some money if I do."

"While a lot of commercial Web sites have referral and affiliate programs that pay money, so far Google doesn't," I said. "But who knows? That might change in the future."

"So why didn't you send *us* referrals?" Anita asked.

I laughed and said, "Because I was dumb! You're right, I should have, in case it's worth something later. Oh well....The referral program is one of those features that was added later, so I've not paid too much attention to it. I'll certainly keep it in mind from now on."

Managing AdSense

"Now let's look more closely at each part of the console," I continued. "Remember, everything about AdSense is automated, so you'll spend a lot of time with the console initially."

"Can you ever talk to a human being?" Anita asked.

"Absolutely," I said, "there's a 'Contact Us' link at the top of the console. Or you can send email directly to adsense-support@google.com and someone will get back to you within one or two business days."

"I've already had contact with them," Stef said, "and they answered my question pretty quickly. The reply was very polite, too, even though they probably get a lot of dumb questions like mine!"

"Well, it's worth their effort to keep the AdSense publishers happy," I replied, "because the more ads get shown by more publishers, the more money Google makes. Remember, this is a *partnership* between you and Google, so it benefits both of you to treat each other well."

Google Referrals

For up-to-date information about Google's referral program, see www.memwg.com/google-referrals.

Be Proactive

The AdSense customer service representatives are happy to answer any questions you have about the program, so contact them for clarification *before* you do anything that might contravene the AdSense program policies.

"So what part of the console should we start with?" Stef asked. "I haven't explored it all in detail."

"That's OK," I said, "we'll figure it out as we go along. Start with the ad reports and we'll go from there."

Stef then went on to describe (with my help) each page in the console.

Reports

The Reports tab consists of two pages: *Ad Performance* and *Search Performance*. The former reports on AdSense for content earnings, the latter on AdSense for search earnings. The pages are otherwise identical.

The controls at the top of the report page define what kind of report is generated. The actual report is shown immediately below the report controls. There are two basic types of report available:

▶ an **aggregate data** report summarizing each day's data

▶ a **channel data** report displaying channel-specific data

With the aggregate data report, you see how much you're actually earning. With the channel data report, you see how well pages or groups of pages are performing.

Overlapping Channels

Pages that are simultaneously in custom channels and URL channels get their clicks and earnings double-counted in channel data reports. When overlapping channels are used, then, the total earnings shown in the channel data report may exceed those shown in the aggregate data report. The aggregate data report is always correct.

A report shows the data between two dates. A number of predefined date ranges are provided (**Figure 7.7**). The "today" and "this month" ranges are usually the most interesting ranges to look at (remember that Google pays AdSense earnings on a monthly basis, providing you earn at least $100 each month). Other ranges can be specified manually using the date controls immediately below the list of predefined ranges.

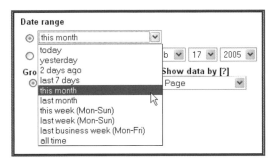

Figure 7.7 Predefined date ranges for easy report generation.

Aggregate reports can show total page impressions or total ad unit impressions. Channel reports are more flexible, allowing you to select precisely which channels you're interested in and how the data for those channels is to be shown—per-date totals, per-channel totals, or a detailed list of channel earnings per day.

After changing the report controls, click the Display Report button below the controls to generate the new report. A typical two-day aggregate report for page impressions is shown in **Figure 7.8**. The data are initially sorted by date, but you can click any column heading to sort by that column. The columns are:

▶ **Date**—the reporting date

▶ **Channel**—the channel (channel reports only)

▶ **Page impressions**—the number of times ads have been shown on a page

- ▸ **Clicks**—the number of valid ad clicks

- ▸ **Page CTR**—the page *clickthrough rate*, the number of clicks divided by the number of impressions

- ▸ **Page eCPM**—the *effective cost per 1000 impressions*, how much money on average each page is earning based on a standard industry unit

- ▸ **Your earnings**—the amount earned

If you choose to view aggregate data for ad unit impressions instead of pages, you will see equivalent column headings (Ad unit impressions, Ad unit CTR, and Ad unit eCPM), with all calculations done using ad units.

Wednesday, February 16, 2005 - Thursday, February 17, 2005					Download CSV file
Date ▾	Page impressions	Clicks	Page CTR	Page eCPM [?]	Your earnings
Wednesday, February 16, 2005	762	11	1.4%	$6.54	$4.98
Thursday, February 17, 2005	685	11	1.6%	$19.34	$13.25
Totals	**1,447**	**22**	**1.5%**	**$12.60**	**$18.23**
Averages	723	11			$9.12

Figure 7.8 A typical aggregate report.

Search Earnings Treated Differently

At the bottom of the search report, you'll see this statement: "Revenue from AdSense for search may be offset at the end of the month by costs associated with performing searches." If a site's visitors do a lot of searching but don't click many ads, the publisher may find that Google has adjusted the site's AdSense for search earnings to recover some of the costs of providing the search service. (AdSense for content earnings are not affected.) This only occurs for a few sites, and the chargeback never exceeds the AdSense for search earnings for that month.

You can download any report to your computer by clicking the Download CSV file link in the top right-hand corner of the report. The downloaded report can then be opened with any spreadsheet application (CSV is a universally supported spreadsheet file format) for further analysis.

Ad Settings

The *Ad Settings* tab consists of four pages: Ad layout code, Ad colors, Channels, and Competitive Ad Filter. The Ad layout code and Ad colors pages are described in detail in the next chapter, so only the Channels and Competitive Ad Filter pages are described here.

You manage your custom and URL channels from the Channels page. At the top of the page are the URL channel controls (**Figure 7.9**). The custom channel controls are at the bottom (**Figure 7.10**). Creating new channels is simple: Just type the URL or the channel name into the appropriate input field and click the "Create new channel" button.

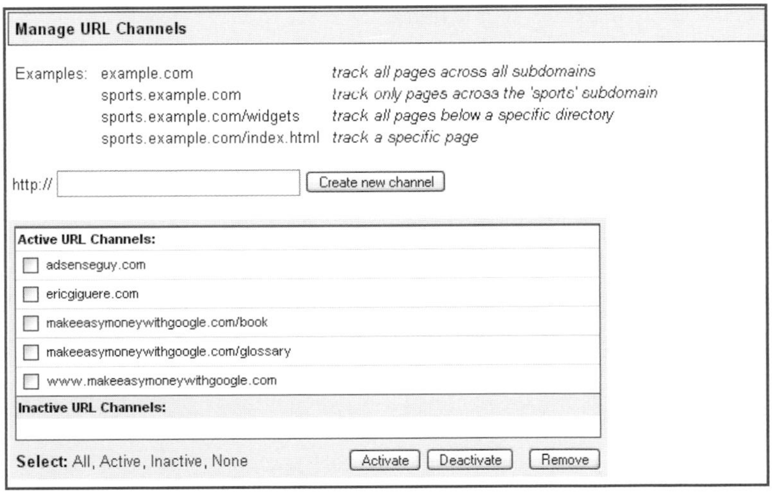

Figure 7.9 Managing URL channels.

Channels

You can have up to 100 active channels at any time—that's more than adequate for most sites.

Ad Filters

For more details on competitive ad filters, see www.memwg.com/ad-filters.

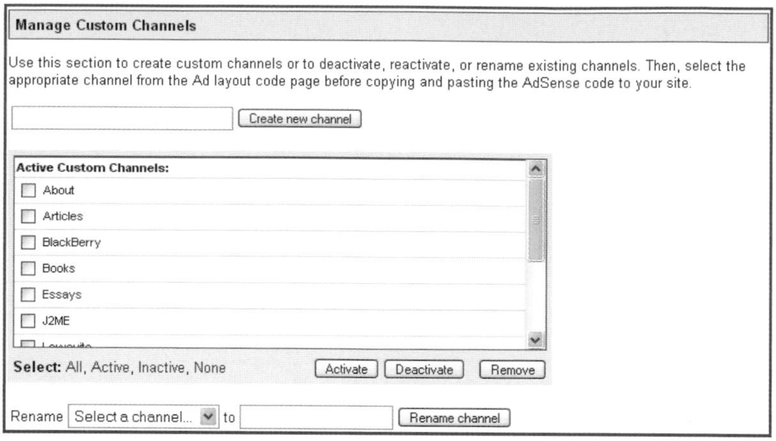

Manage Custom Channels

Use this section to create custom channels or to deactivate, reactivate, or rename existing channels. Then, select the appropriate channel from the Ad layout code page before copying and pasting the AdSense code to your site.

[   ] [Create new channel]

Active Custom Channels:
- [ ] About
- [ ] Articles
- [ ] BlackBerry
- [ ] Books
- [ ] Essays
- [ ] J2ME

Select: All, Active, Inactive, None   [Activate] [Deactivate] [Remove]

Rename [Select a channel... ▾] to [   ] [Rename channel]

Figure 7.10 Managing custom channels.

A channel can be *active* or *inactive*. AdSense tracks only active channels for reporting.

Ad filtering is done from the Competitive Ad Filter page (**Figure 7.11**). Just list the Web addresses you want filtered. Up to 200 addresses can be filtered at any time. This is one area where the AdSense Preview Tool comes in handy: If you see an ad you'd like to filter while using the tool, you can just select the ad and click the Show Selected URLs link on the tool to see the ad's destination address. Copy the address to the clipboard and then paste it right into the ad filter list.

Search Settings

The *Search Settings* tab is very similar to the Ad Settings tab and consists of four pages: Search code, Styles, Channels, and Competitive Ad Filter. The Search code and Styles pages are described in the next chapter. The other two pages are basically identical to their counterparts on the Ad Settings tab. Note that AdSense for search supports only custom channels, not URL channels.

```
┌─────────────────────────────────────────────────────────────────────┐
│ Your Competitive Ad Filters                                           │
├─────────────────────────────────────────────────────────────────────┤
│                                                                       │
│ Examples:  example.com                   block all ads across all subdomains        │
│            sports.example.com            block only ads across the 'sports' subdomain │
│            sports.example.com/widgets    block all ads below a specific directory    │
│            sports.example.com/index.html block all ads for a specific page          │
│                                                                       │
│ Please enter one URL per line (64 character limit per URL, 200 URLs maximum)        │
│ ┌─────────────────────────────────────────────────────────────────┐ │
│ │                                                                   │ │
│ │                                                                   │ │
│ │                                                                   │ │
│ │                                                                   │ │
│ │                                                                   │ │
│ │                                                                   │ │
│ │                                                                   │ │
│ │                                                                   │ │
│ │                                                                   │ │
│ └─────────────────────────────────────────────────────────────────┘ │
│                                                                       │
│ [ Save changes ]  [ Cancel ]                                          │
└─────────────────────────────────────────────────────────────────────┘
```

Figure 7.11 Filtering competitive ads.

Separate Channel and Filter Lists

The AdSense for search channel and filter lists are separate from the AdSense for content channel and filter lists, so changes to one do not affect the other. If you're blocking sites and using both AdSense services, remember to update both lists.

My Account

The *My Accounts* tab consists of three pages: Account Settings, Payment History, and Tax information.

The Account Settings page manages general account settings:

▶ **Login Information**—email address (which can't be changed), password, language choice (the AdSense console is available in different languages), and whether Google has permission to mail you anything other than routine service announcements

▶ **Payee Information**—the name and address to use for payment

▶ **Payment Details**—how the payment is to be made

▶ **Payment Holding**—temporarily suspends payments

▶ **Ad Type Preference**—whether or not image ads are allowed on pages by default (this can be changed on a page-by-page basis)

▶ **Product Subscriptions**—whether you're signed up for both AdSense for content and AdSense for search or just AdSense for content

A typical Accounts Settings page, with important details blurred out, is shown in **Figure 7.12**. Note that edit links are available to change most of the information.

The Payment History page summarizes your monthly earnings and the payments you've been sent (**Figure 7.13**). There is one entry per month for earnings, but payments may occur less frequently if you haven't reached the minimum payment threshold ($100) or you've temporarily suspended payment. Clicking any Earnings or Payment link shows you more details about that month's earnings or payment. Details of earnings for both AdSense for content and AdSense for search are included under Earnings (**Figure 7.14**).

Figure 7.12 Viewing account settings.

Figure 7.13 Payment history.

Tax Help

Consult a tax professional for clarification if you have any questions about which Google Tax Information form to use or about any other tax issue related to AdSense.

Payment History > **Nov 1, 2004 - Nov 30, 2004 Earnings Details**

Download CSV file

Description	**Amount**
AdSense for search	$0.87
AdSense for content	$249.60
Subtotal	$250.47
Total Monthly Earnings	$250.47

Figure 7.14 Earnings details.

The Tax Information page is where Google collects the tax-related information required by the United States government (**Figure 7.15**). The form you use depends on your citizenship, your country of residence, and other factors. A wizard is available to help you select the correct form.

U.S. tax law requires that Google collect tax-related information from all AdSense publishers. Our records indicate that you have already submitted the appropriate information. You are solely responsible for providing and maintaining accurate tax information associated with your account. Google may share this information with trusted third-parties for the purpose of verifying your identity. Should your tax information change, you may resubmit your tax forms at any time. Thank you for your cooperation.

Already know what form to fill in?
Click the correct form name below:

- IRS Form W-9
- Foreign publisher with no U.S. Activities
- IRS Form W-8 ECI
- IRS Form W-8 BEN
- IRS Form W-8 EXP
- IRS Form W-8 IMY
- IRS Form 8233

Or, use this wizard to find the correct form:
Are you a U.S. person (for example a U.S. corporation, a U.S. partnership, a U.S. citizen or a U.S. resident alien)?

Yes (Form W-9)
No

Continue >>

Please note that the tax information collection interface and any tax-related information provided by Google is not intended as and should not be construed as legal, tax, or investment advice. You should always consult your tax advisor to help answer specific questions regarding how tax laws apply to you and/or your business. The tax summary we have provided is necessarily incomplete, and the tax laws and regulations are subject to change. Therefore, Google does not guarantee and is not liable for the accuracy or completeness of any tax information provided, or any results or outcome as a result of the use of this information. For specific information regarding U.S. tax requirements, please visit the IRS website located at http://www.irs.gov.

Google uses industry-standard SSL (secure socket layer) technology to protect this and other personal information you provide us. In addition, taxpayer ID numbers are stored in encrypted format for additional security. Please read the Google Privacy Policy for more information about what we do to protect your privacy.

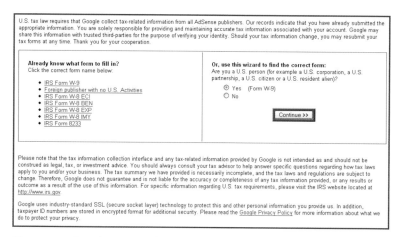

Figure 7.15 Supplying Google with tax-related information.

Getting Paid

"If you only get paid when your earnings reach $100," Claude asked, "how many months does a new AdSense publisher have to wait to be paid?"

"There aren't any statistics available," I answered, "and it really depends on how much traffic the site is getting and how much money you're getting per click. My first site had pretty low traffic initially, so it took me a few months to get my first payment. And back then, Google always paid out accounts at the end of the calendar year, even if they had accumulated earnings less than $100. I don't think Stef will earn $100 this month, but $10 in a couple of weeks is a good start."

"When do you actually get paid?" Stef asked.

"Google sends the payments about a month after you've earned them," I said. "They're very consistent with their schedule."

"They send you a check?" Claude said.

"Yes," I said. "International publishers can even get paid in other currencies. You can get the check sent by courier to you if you're in a hurry. Alternatively, you can now sign up for EFT—electronic fund transfer."

"And have the money deposited directly into your bank account," Claude said.

"You choose your payment type from the Account Settings page," I said. "It's really easy. I still get checks—it's nice to physically receive them. But if I were making several thousand dollars a month from AdSense, I'd probably want to get the money more quickly, and I'd either get the check by courier or use EFT."

Reality Check

"Do sites really make several thousand a month?" Claude wondered.

"There are sites that claim they do," I said. "It's all a numbers game. With a lot of traffic and a lot of clickthroughs, anything's possible. But don't count on making that kind of money."

"Speaking of which," said Claude, "isn't it time we learn how we make *any* money? I know Stef's figured it all out, but I'd like some more details."

"Which brings us to part two of our session, how to place ads on your site," I replied. "That *is* the really interesting part, so let's get started."

chapter eight

Publishing Ads on Your Site

> Claude: This is the part where it gets exciting. It seems like I've waited forever to get to this stage.

> Eric: If you were an experienced Web site developer, AdSense ads would be simple to add to your site. Really, they're simple to add no matter what your experience level. The hard part is figuring out what ad formats to use and where to place them on your Web pages.

> Stef: And you can help there, right?

> Eric: I can help a bit, sure, but ultimately it's up to you to figure out what works best for your site and your audience. It may take you a while and some experimentation to do it.

"This is the part where it gets exciting," Claude said. "It seems like I've waited forever to get to this stage."

"That's because you had to learn a lot of new stuff, Dad," said Anita. "We all had to. We had to crawl before we could run."

"That's right," I told Claude, "and if you were an experienced Web site developer, AdSense ads would be simple to add to your site. Really, they're simple to add no matter what your experience level. There's no mystery to becoming an AdSense publisher. The hard part is figuring out *what* ad formats to use and *where* to place them on your Web pages."

"And you can help there, right?" Stef asked. "The ads were easy to put on my blog, but I didn't do any experimenting. I just followed the instructions that Blogger gave me."

"I can help a bit, sure," I said, "but ultimately it's up to you to figure out what works best for your site and your audience. It may take you a while and some experimentation to do it."

Claude was eager to get going. "I don't know if I can run yet," he said, "but I'm certainly willing to walk."

I turned to Stef. "Let's start with you again, Stef," I said. "Why don't you show us what you did to publish ads on your blog?"

Adding the Code

"It really wasn't a big deal to do," Stef said. "Blogger's instructions were easy to follow. First you log in to your AdSense account and go to the Ad layout code page." Since we were still logged in to my account, Stef merely clicked on the Ad Settings tab to bring up the *Ad layout code page* (**Figure 8.1**). "As you can see, this is a long page with many options. The options don't all fit in the window—you have to scroll down to see them, like this." Stef revealed the rest of the page (**Figure 8.2**).

Figure 8.1 The top of the Ad layout code page.

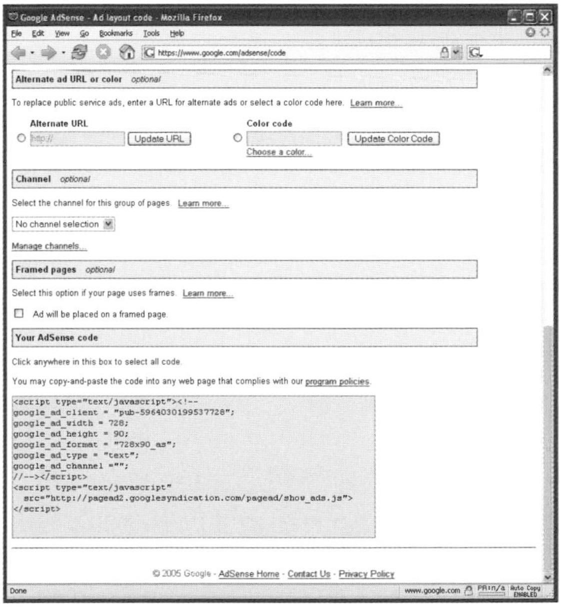

Figure 8.2 The bottom of the Ad layout code page.

Ad Pixels

The dimensions of the ads refer to the ad's width and height in pixels. Many Web pages are designed to be 800 pixels wide by 600 pixels high, so a 120-by-600 vertical banner runs the whole height of a typical site.

"It looks a bit intimidating when you see it all," Anita said.

"I thought so, too," Stef continued, "but it's not that bad. All you really have to do to get started is choose the ad format—what they call an ad layout—and a color scheme—which they call a color palette. I chose one of the skyscraper layouts because I was putting the ads in the blog sidebar. So let's do that now, too." Stef chose the 120 x 600 Skyscraper format from the drop-down list of ad layouts (**Figure 8.3**).

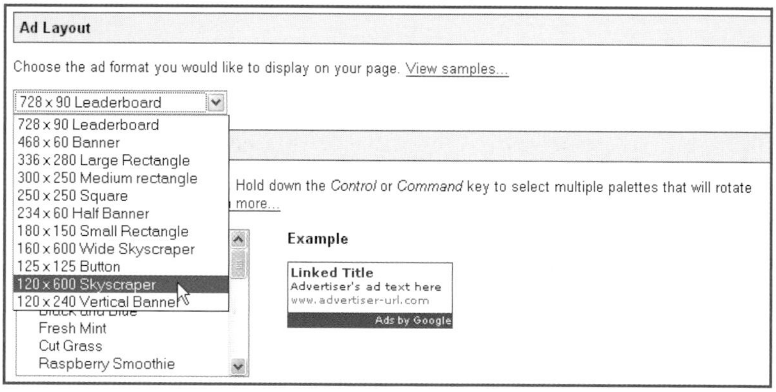

Figure 8.3 Choosing an ad layout.

"The 120 by 600 refers to the size of the ads?" Anita asked.

"Yes, the width and the height of the entire ad block, in that order," Stef answered. "You have to choose the format that fits your page layout, of course. Then I chose the color scheme, one that looked good with my blog's color scheme. I wasn't sure if I should make the ads stand out or not, so I chose something complementary."

"Let's pretend you're working with a light blue background for this, Stef," I said. "What scheme would you choose?"

Stef scrolled through the list of colors. "Hmm…if I wanted the ads to blend in, I could choose this one," she said, selecting Melancholy Blue from the list (**Figure 8.4**).

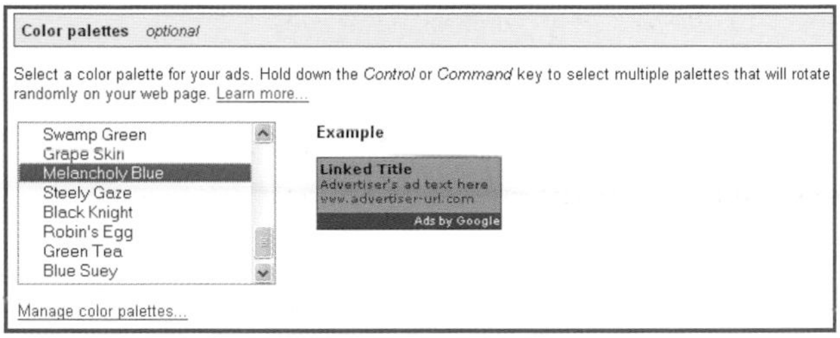

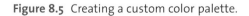

Figure 8.4 Choosing a color palette.

"Hey, the sample ad changed colors!" Claude noticed.

"Or I could choose one that really contrasts with the background," Stef continued, clicking on each color palette in the list. "Looks like I'll have to create my own color scheme," she said as she clicked the "Manage color palettes" link. "You do that on the Ad colors page." Stef had temporarily left the Ad layout page in order to create her new color scheme (**Figure 8.5**). "I had to create my own palette because I didn't really like Google's color schemes."

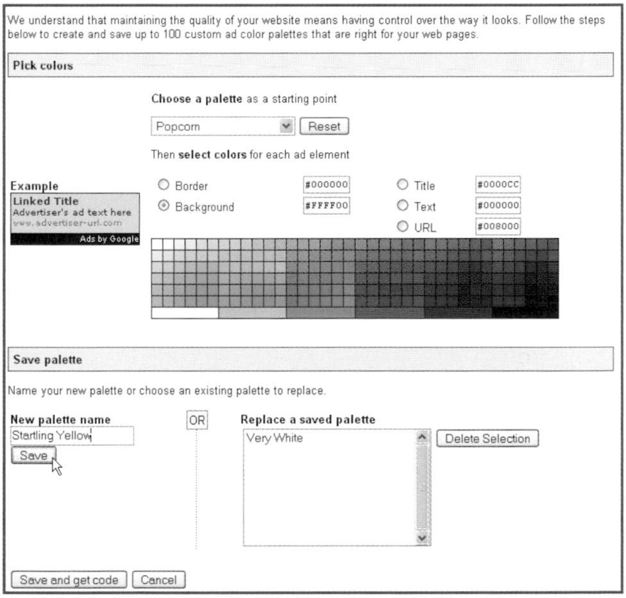

Figure 8.5 Creating a custom color palette.

"They're not very bold for the most part," I agreed.

"And I can be pretty bold sometimes," Stef continued. "So let's create a bright yellow ad with a nice black border….There we go! I'll call it Startling Yellow and save it." Stef clicked the button marked "Save and get code," which returned her to the Ad layout code page. "Now I choose my new custom palette and scroll to the bottom of the page. There's the code to display the ads." Stef clicked in the box labeled "Your AdSense code" to automatically select the code (**Figure 8.6**).

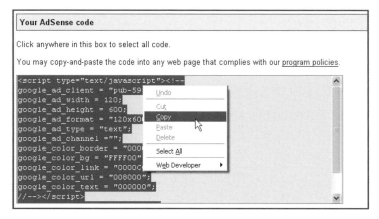

Figure 8.6 Selecting and copying the AdSense code to the clipboard.

After copying the code to the clipboard, Stef turned to me. "Do you want me to go to Blogger and show how to add the code to a blog?" she asked.

"No, let's just use a simple Web page," I said. "Start up Nvu and create a page with a light blue background and some text."

"OK," she said, quickly creating a new page called `simple.html` (**Figure 8.7**). "So I guess now I can paste the code…oops, that doesn't seem to work!" The code was now showing *on* the page (**Figure 8.8**). "Better undo that…."

"Switch to the Source view and paste the code there," I suggested.

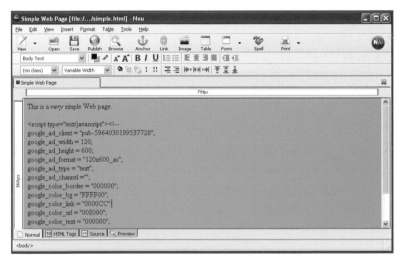

Figure 8.7 Creating a simple page.

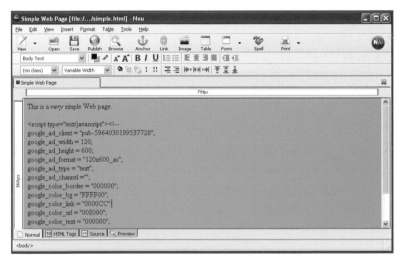

Figure 8.8 The wrong place to paste the code.

"Right!" Stef exclaimed. "That makes sense—that's what I did with my blog. I had to go paste the code between the body tags. I'll add the code to the end of the body." Switching to the Source view, she repasted the code (**Figure 8.9**).

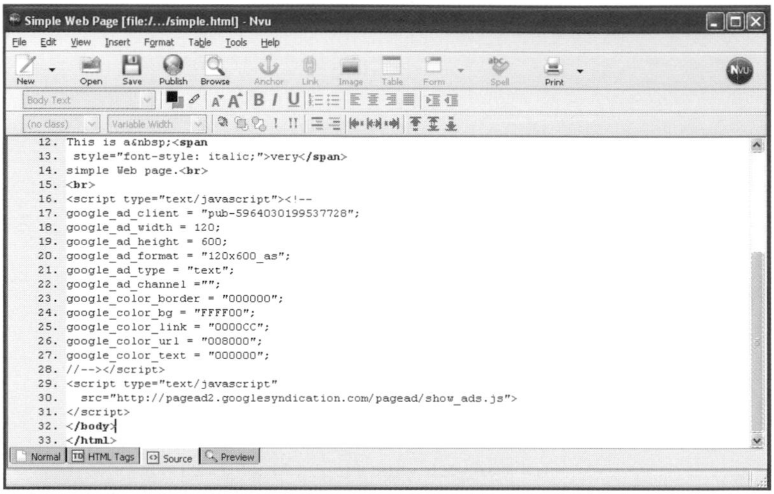

Figure 8.9 Pasting the code into the Source view.

"There!" she said. "Now let's preview the page….Nothing! Where are the ads? The ads on my blog showed up right away!"

"That's because Nvu skips over the JavaScript code," I explained. "Save the file and hit the Browse button instead." She did, and a new browser window opened (**Figure 8.10**).

"There they are!" said Anita excitedly.

"AdSense is showing an ad for voice-over-IP," Claude said. "How did it figure that out?"

"The code looks at the page's address and sends it along to Google's servers," I said. "Stef saved the file in the same folder we used before: VoIP-at-home. Look at the address bar in the browser."

Figure 8.10 Testing the ad code.

"And that's how it matched a VoIP ad to the page—clever!" said Claude.

"But most of the time you're *not* going to see any ads until you place the page up on your Web server," I continued. "Or you may see PSAs."

"What are those again?" Claude asked.

"Public service announcements—ads for charitable causes," I answered. "But you can disable those if you want from the code layout page."

"That page doesn't look very good," Stef said. "I should have used a banner ad instead."

"Oh, I know how to fix that," said Anita. "Can I have the keyboard, Stef? Thanks." Typing quickly, she inserted a table definition right into the HTML code.

"I see you've been practicing!" I said.

Using Tables

An interesting discussion of when and why to use tables, even in a CSS page, can be found at www.memwg.com/ using-tables/.

"You wouldn't believe how much time I've spent trying to get the layout of my site just right," Anita said. "I learned a few things doing it. This may not be the best way to do it, but if you use a single-row table and place the content in the left cell and the ads in the right cell, you get a two-column effect like this." She saved her changes and reloaded the page (**Figure 8.11**).

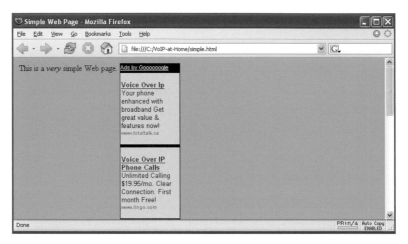

Figure 8.11 Changing the page layout.

"Oh, I believe you," I told her. "A good layout can be hard to do. I've often resorted to tables myself. Purists don't like it, but you want your site to look good. Although I must point out that you *can* do the column effect you want with style sheets. In any case, once the code's pasted into the page, you just place the modified page up on your Web site and load it once into your browser. Shortly after, AdSense will crawl the page to analyze its content—if you don't see relevant ads right away, you'll see them within an hour or so."

"It was very cool," Stef said. "And I had to stop myself from clicking some of the ads."

"That's right, and it bears repeating: *Don't click the ads on your site no matter what*," I said. "Otherwise, Google may think you're performing click fraud and they could kick you out of the program."

I stood up. "OK, let's take a quick break," I said, "and then we'll look at the Ad layout code page in more detail."

SSI

Server Side Includes (SSI) techniques are covered in more detail at www.memwg.com/ server-side-includes.

Tweaking the Code

After the break, I took control of the computer. "As you just saw, publishing ads on your site is actually very simple," I began. "And the basics never change: Set the options you want, copy the generated code to the clipboard, paste the code into your Web pages. All we're going to do now is tweak the code."

"What do you mean?" Claude asked.

"I mean, I'm going to change some of the options on the Ad layout code page," I said, "and see how it affects the code and the ads that are displayed."

"So every time you want to make a change," Anita asked, "you have to go and repaste the code into all your pages?"

"Yes," I admitted, "*unless* your Web server supports some kind of template feature the way blogs do. This is usually called *server-side includes,* and it lets you place the AdSense code in a separate file and have it included automatically in all your Web pages."

"Like the style sheet," Stef said.

"Yes, the same idea," I agreed. "But how it's done really depends on what Web server you're using—you need to talk to your hosting service provider to get the details. The end result is the same, but whenever you want to update the AdSense code, you just change one file on your site instead of changing each Web page."

"So let's see you do some tweaking," Claude said.

"OK, we'll go through each section of the Ad layout code page, starting at the top."

Ad Type

You specify what kind of ad you want to use with the *Ad type* section (**Figure 8.12**). There are two basic types of ads to choose:

▶ **Ad units,** for conventional text or image ads

▶ **Ad links units,** for links to a page of text ads

The standard ad unit can display either text or image ads or both (though images can be displayed only in certain ad formats), so you must indicate which kinds of ads to display.

If you're using an ad link unit, select how many links you want displayed in each unit.

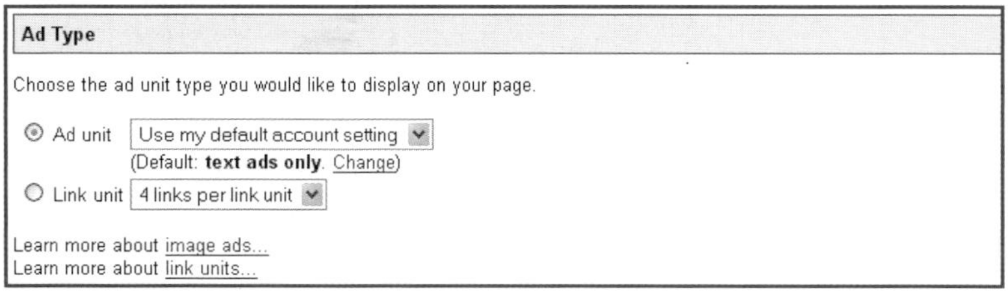

Figure 8.12 Selecting the ad type.

Ad Layout

The *Ad layout* section selects the ad format (**Figure 8.13**). The available formats vary depending on the ad type. Standard ad units support the formats pictured in **Figures 8.14** to **8.24**.

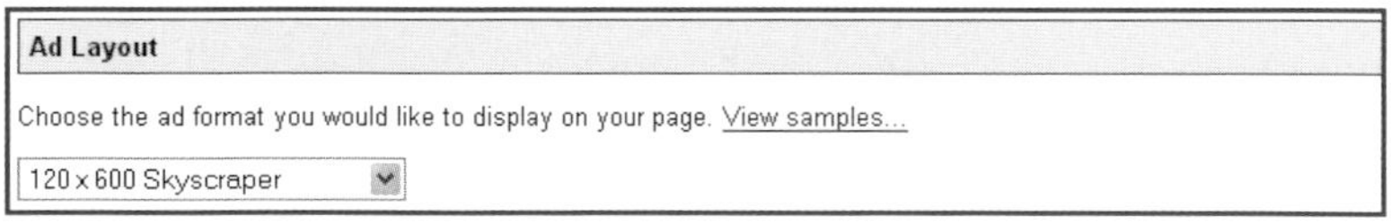

Figure 8.13 Selecting the ad format.

Figure 8.14 The leaderboard (728 x 90) format.

Telephone Solutions
TeleVantage, VoIP Calls Customized
Interactive IVR

Voice Over Ip
Your phone enhanced with broadband
Get great value & features now!

Ads by Goooooogle

Figure 8.15 The banner (468 x 60) format.

Figure 8.16 The half banner (234 x 60) format.

Figure 8.17 The button (125 x 125) format.

Figure 8.20 The vertical banner (120 x 240) format.

Figure 8.18 The skyscraper (120 x 600) format.

Figure 8.19 The wide skyscraper (160 x 600) format.

New Ad Formats

New ad formats are added from time to time, so check www.memwg.com/ad-formats for updates.

Figure 8.21
The small rectangle (180 x 150) format.

Figure 8.22 The square (250 x 250) format.

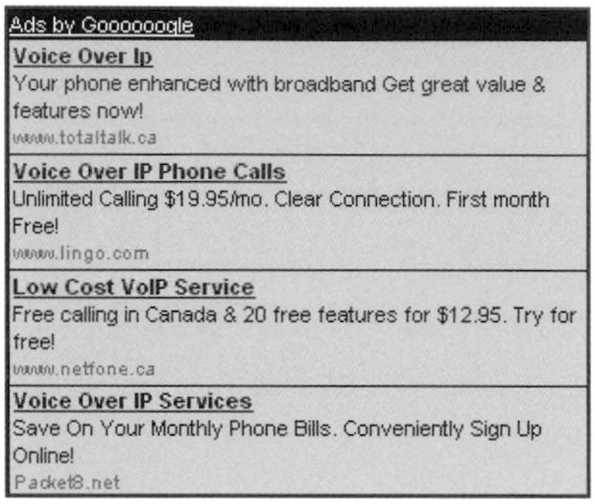

Figure 8.23 The medium rectangle (300 x 250) format.

Figure 8.24 The large rectangle (336 x 280) format.

As you can see, there's a wide variety of ad unit formats to choose from.

Ad links units support four formats: 120 x 90, 160 x 90, 180 x 90, and 200 x 90. A four-line 120 x 90 format is shown in **Figure 8.25**, and the same size but with five lines is shown in **Figure 8.26**.

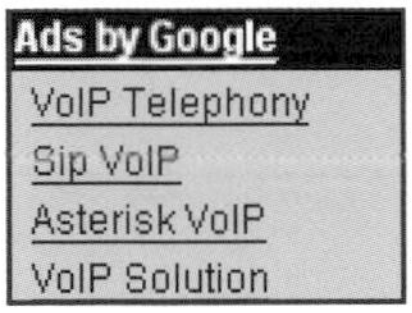

Figure 8.25
A four-line ad links unit.

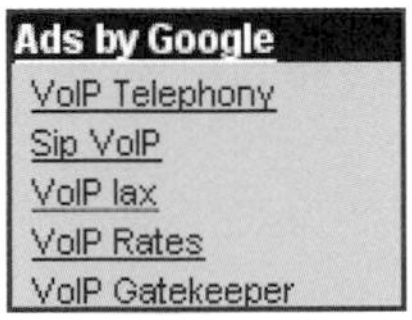

Figure 8.26
A five-line ad links unit.

Color Palette

The *Color palettes* section selects the colors used by the text ads from a set of predefined and custom color schemes (**Figure 8.27**). All palette management (creating, editing, or deleting custom palettes) is done from the Ad colors page.

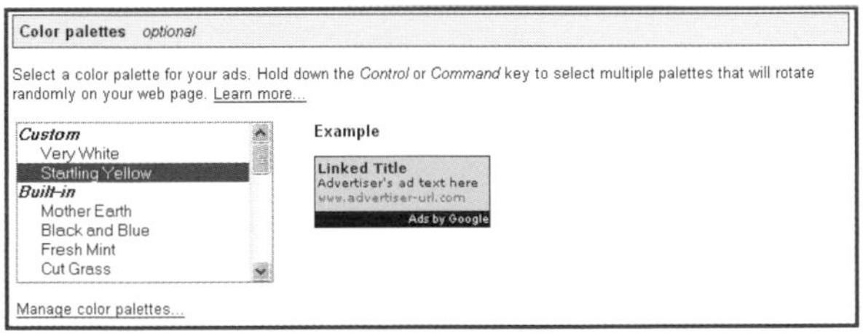

Figure 8.27 Selecting the color palette.

Alternate Ad

If you want to avoid displaying PSAs (public service ads), you can use the *Alternate ad URL or color* section to specify an alternate ad, image, or color (**Figure 8.28**) which will take their place on the page. For ads or images, enter the Web address and click the Update code button. For example, if Claude were using a banner (468 x 60) format

Alternate Ads

For more advanced
alternate ad and PSA-
avoidance techniques,
see www.memwg.com/
alternate-ads.

he could avoid PSAs by creating an identically sized image for his
Web site and setting the alternate ad URL as follows:

```
http://www.voip-at-home.com/images/
alternate_ad_468_60.gif
```

Whenever a PSA would otherwise be displayed, the AdSense code
would simply display this image. You can even embed small Web
pages with links and images or display ads from another (non-
competing) ad service.

Figure 8.28 Specifying an alternate ad.

If you don't have an alternate ad or image, you can still avoid PSAs
by clicking the "Choose a color" link and selecting an appropriate
background color from the resulting pop-up window (**Figure 8.29**).
Don't forget to click the Update code button after dismissing the
pop-up window. The AdSense code is updated to fill the area of the
ad unit with the background color you chose whenever PSAs would
otherwise be displayed.

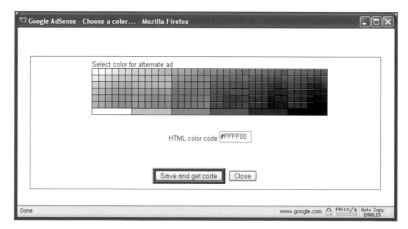

Figure 8.29 Choosing an alternate color.

Channel

The *Channel* section assigns a custom channel to the AdSense code (**Figure 8.30**). All pages that include the code will have their impressions and clicks recorded under the selected channel.

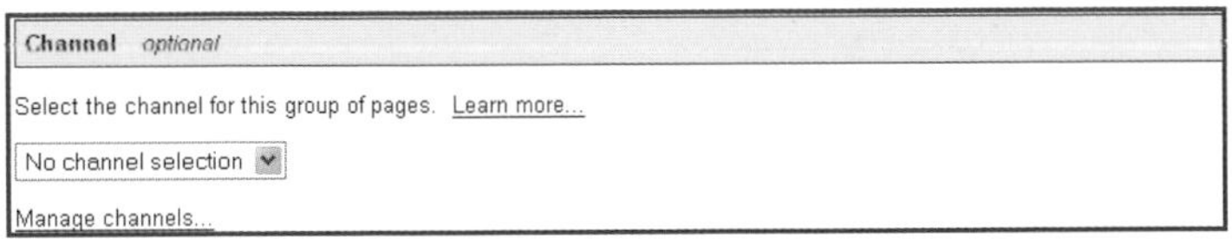

Figure 8.30 Selecting a custom channel.

Note that this section of the layout code page deals only with custom channels, since URL channels are defined without changing the AdSense code.

More on Frames

Frames aren't used much these days, having been largely replaced by CSS and SSI, so for more information see www.memwg.com/frames.

Framing

Finally, the *Framed pages* section (**Figure 8.31**) tells AdSense that you're using frames. This is an advanced way to split a Web page into multiple parts (the frames), each of which displays another Web page. If frames are used, the AdSense code needs to change slightly to find the correct content; hence the need for this section.

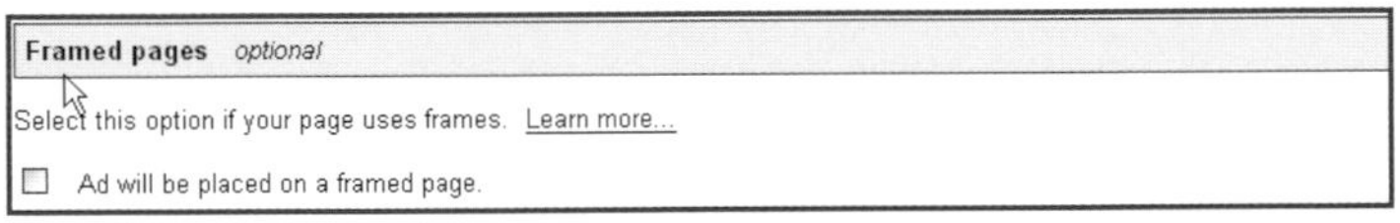

Figure 8.31 Specifying that frames are used.

The Code

The *Your AdSense code* section is where the management console places the generated AdSense code. Don't modify this code; Google checks sites at random to see if the generated code is intact. Once you're done tweaking the options, copy the code to the clipboard and paste it into your Web pages.

The code isn't stored anywhere in the console or on Google's pages (although it is stored on your own pages once you've pasted it in). If you close the console page and you need to regenerate the code at a future point (for instance, if you want to change your ad layout), you'll have to reset all the code layout options. It would be prudent to write down important settings for the future.

Placing the Ads

"Wow," said Anita, "there are a lot of ad formats to choose from. I count, what, eleven of them?"

"So far, yes," I said. "When I first started using AdSense, there were only four. And the ad links are much more recent additions. Definitely lots to choose from."

"Do they all get used?" Stef asked. "All the blogs I've seen with ads put them on the side, like I did."

"I think they all get used, yes," I answered, "but I think certain formats are much more popular than others. Certainly the tower formats—especially the original skyscraper layout—are popular. They fit naturally on the left or right side of a page. Of course, the banners work well at the top or bottom of the page, in the header or footer."

"The button format would work well in a corner," Anita said.

"And the others can be inserted right into the middle of your content," I said.

"Is that a good idea?" Claude asked. "Doesn't it interfere with the flow of the text?"

"I see it all the time on some sites," Anita said. "Not necessarily AdSense ads, but other kinds of ads. Sometimes they *do* interfere."

"You have to strike a balance," I said. "You *want* the ads noticed, otherwise nobody will click on them. That's why many sites use contrasting colors for the ads. But if you have a page full of ads and very little content, your visitors won't be happy and they're just as likely to leave by hitting the browser's Back button."

"How many ads should you place on the page, then?" Anita asked.

"I know!" Claude said. "Put them in the header and the footer and on each side. That won't interfere with the reading."

"You can't, Claude," I told him, "because Google limits you to using no more than three ad or ad links units per page. You also can't place ads on certain pages, like pages that have no real content. Error pages, such as the 'page not found' errors you get when you mistype a page address, have no real content, for example."

"I think a page surrounded by ads would be ugly anyhow, Dad," Anita said. "And there'd be no room for anything else!"

"All right, but how do you put multiple units on a single page?" Claude asked.

"You just copy the generated code into two or three different spots on the page," I said. "It's not a big deal."

"Can we see sample ad placements?" Anita asked.

"Yes," I said, "there are two ways to do that. Google has some samples up on its site, available from `www.google.com/adsense/adformats`. However, if you want to see actual examples on real Web sites, there's a trick you can do with Google." I pointed to the generated code in the browser window. "If you look in the generated code, you'll see a line that starts with 'google_ad_format,' followed by a value in quotes. That's the internal name that AdSense uses for the ad format you've chosen. Just search for that string using Google and you'll get a list of sites that are displaying those kinds of ads."

"Ah! That's because the code is *in* the Web pages and Google indexes them, too!" Stef said.

"Right," I agreed. "And if you ever find a site that looks really good and you want to see how they're doing it, use the View source or Page source option on your browser to see the raw HTML for the page." I browsed to my personal site and showed them the source HTML of the home page (**Figure 8.32**).

```
Source of: http://www.ericgiguere.com/index.html - Mozilla Firefox
File   Edit   View
<!DOCTYPE HTML PUBLIC "-//W3C//DTD HTML 4.0 Transitional//EN">
<html>
<head>
<title>EricGiguere.com</title>
<meta name="description" content="A site promoting books, articles a
<meta name="keywords" content="Eric Giguere, J2ME, Java, palm, palm
<link rel="stylesheet" type="text/css" href="/stylesheet.css;jsessio
</head>
<body bgcolor="#FFFFFF" text="#000000" link="#0000cc"
      vlink="551A8B" alink="#FF0000">
<div align="center">
<table cellpadding="0" cellspacing="0" border="0" width="840">
```

Figure 8.32 Viewing the HTML of a Web page from within the browser.

Adding Search Code

"Speaking of search," Stef said, "how do you add a Google search box to a page?"

"It's just as easy as adding the ads," I said. "You go to the Search Settings tab and then the Search code page." I logged back into the AdSense console and went to the Search code page (**Figure 8.33**). "As you can see, it's similar to the Ad layout code page we just saw."

"There seem to be more options," Stef said.

"There are," I agreed, "because the search box must be customized for your site. You have to tell it what language to use for searching and which Google search engine to use, among other things."

"I thought there was only one Google search engine?" Claude asked.

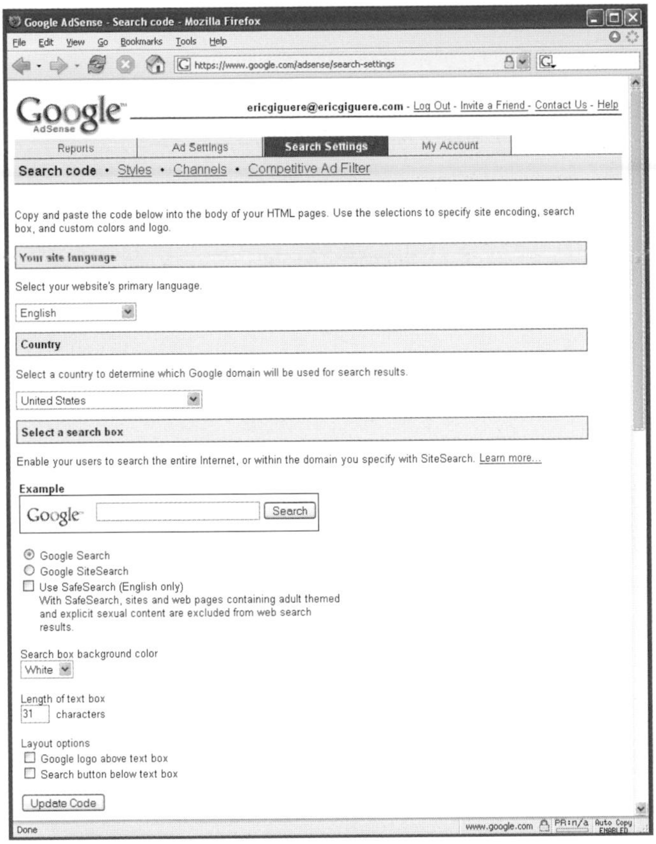

Figure 8.33 Part of the Search code page.

¿Se habla Google?

Search specific languages and countries in Google from www.googlc.com/language_tools.

"Google actually runs country-specific search sites like www.google.ca or www.google.fr," I explained. "The search engine technology is the same, but the country-specific search sites rank sites differently."

"The 'Select a search box' section looks pretty complicated," Anita suggested.

"It's not that bad," I assured her. "Basically, you're telling Google how the search box should look and what domains it should search. Besides doing a general Web search, the search box can restrict itself to searching just your own site." I clicked on the Google SiteSearch radio button (**Figure 8.34**). "See how you can enter a domain name? Let's create a search box to search Claude's site."

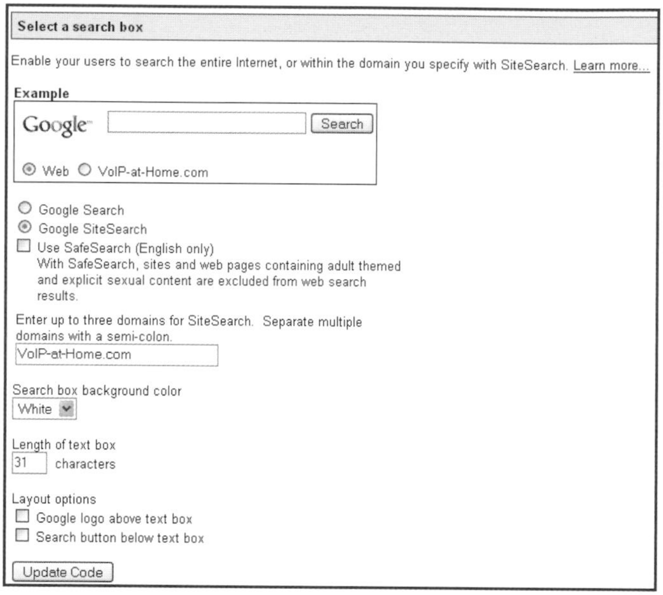

Figure 8.34 Creating a site-specific search box.

"All we do now is select a style palette for the results window," I continued. "Basically, this controls the look of the search-results window—the window you get after clicking the search box's Search button. You can tailor the window to match your own site's color scheme and even include a logo. You use the Styles page to manage the style palettes, but we'll just use one of the predefined ones for this example. There. Now you do just like before with the ads—you select the code at the bottom, copy it to the clipboard, and paste it into a Web page."

After copying the code, I used Nvu to create a new page and pasted the code into the page body. After publishing the page to Claude's site, I loaded it into the browser (**Figure 8.35**).

"There's the search box," I said. "It works immediately." I typed the phrase "voip" into the box and clicked the Search button. A search-results page was displayed (**Figure 8.36**).

Figure 8.35 The finished search box.

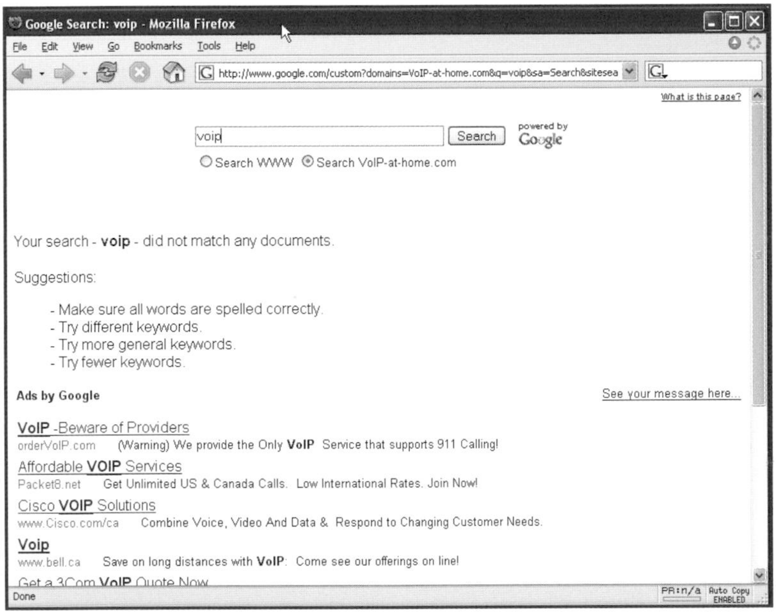

Figure 8.36 The search-results page.

"So I'll make money if someone clicks on those ads?" Claude asked.

"Just like you would with ads on your site, yes," I said. "And the same warning applies: Don't click the ads yourself!"

Tips and Tricks

Stef looked closely at the search-results page. "But it says that the search didn't match any documents," Stef asked. "Why not? Every page on his site should match that search phrase—it's a site about voice-over-IP, after all."

"That's because his site's not in Google's search index yet," I said. "We'll have to fix that, but let's leave that for our next session. Instead, I'd like to give you some tips and tricks about using AdSense on your Web pages."

Only Put Ads on Finished Pages

AdSense is notified whenever AdSense code runs on a page. If AdSense has never seen a page before, it dispatches the AdSense Web crawler to fetch and analyze the page's content. If the page is unfinished, the crawler may not accurately determine the page's topic, though it can infer things based on its analysis of other pages on the same site. Worse still, if the page is full of dummy or otherwise off-topic content, the crawler may get the topic completely wrong.

The moral of this story? Don't put ads on unfinished pages.

Rename Pages to Solve Ad Problems

What if you have a page and the ads aren't relevant because you had poor or empty content on the page when the crawler first came along? While the initial crawling occurs pretty quickly, it may be days or weeks before the AdSense crawler revisits a page and notices that the content is different. In the meantime, you're stuck with irrelevant ads.

The solution is to move the content to another Web page entirely. Make sure the new page is named properly and that its content is correct. Keep the old page around, but have it *redirect* browsers to the new page. A redirect tells the browser that the page has "moved" to a new Web address. Here's a very simple Web page that redirects the browser to another page:

```
<html><head><title>This page has moved</title>
<meta http-equiv="refresh" content="0; url=newpage.html">
</head><body>
This page has <a href="newpage.html">moved to
newpage.html</a>.
</body></html>
```

The redirection is actually done by the *meta* tag. The body of the HTML page is there in case the user's browser doesn't automatically follow redirects and has a direct link to the new page as well.

Redirection can also be done automatically by the Web server. Talk to your hosting service provider about how to do this.

Move Ads Above the Fold

Ads that are not shown "above the fold" (in the top part of the page) won't be seen by visitors unless and until they scroll the page. Placing a single ad unit at the bottom of the page will not generate much revenue. Unless you're using multiple ad units, keep the ads above the fold as much as possible.

Avoid Empty Ad Units

When using multiple ad units on a page, be sure to specify alternate ads or colors for the second and/or third units. The less popular topics don't always have enough ads available to fill two or three units. An empty ad unit is worse than a partially filled one, so always specify a background color or an alternate ad to display in its place. This is a good strategy with *all* your ad units, in fact, even if they're the only ones on the page.

Don't Use Too Many Ads

The presence of too many ads on a page detracts from the page content and may cause visitors to ignore the page entirely, especially if they're looking for objective sources of information. This is particularly a problem if the page is being forced out of its natural shape in order to display as many ads as possible.

Ad Unit Order Matters

The order in which ad units are declared in the underlying HTML determines the order that AdSense uses to fill them. The primary ad unit is the first one declared in your HTML. You want it to be located in the most effective spot on your page, because it's the one that AdSense always fills first and that you expect to always show at least one ad. If you're not careful, the primary ad unit might end up in an ineffective position on your page.

The position of a text ad depends on how much the advertiser is willing to pay when someone clicks it. The ads in the first ad unit—the topmost ads in towers and rectangles and the leftmost ads in banners—pay you more than the other ads, and those in the last ad unit (at the bottom or the extreme right) pay the least.

Use Channels to Track Performance

Channels allow you to see which pages are generating revenue and which aren't. For a small site of less than 100 pages, you can use individual channels (URL channels are simplest) to track performance at the page level. Beyond that, you'll need to group pages together for tracking, probably using custom channels. Once you know which pages are working best, try to figure out why they are and how you can extend that success to other pages.

Don't Put Ads on Private Pages

You can easily create private Web pages on your site that are accessible only by password. There's no point in putting ads on private pages, because the AdSense crawler can read only public pages that anyone can access.

Putting It into Practice

"Well, I can't wait to put all this into practice!" said Claude. He *did* seem pretty excited. "I should be able to get ads up on my pages in no time. I think I'll go for the standard vertical ones—I left some room for those already. But those ad links also look interesting. Maybe I'll throw them into a corner of the page...."

"I'm not sure I'm going to do anything different from what I'm already doing," said Stef. "Except maybe put in some channels—it'd be nice to know which of my pages are making me money. I have such a variety of topics in my blog. Do channels work with blogs, too?"

"Sure, URL channels can work quite well," I said. "It really depends on how your blogging software stores the entries. Just remember to define the channels based on the permanent pages—the *permalink* ones—and not the blog's main page."

I looked at my watch. "Look how late it is again!" I said. "I think we should wrap it up for now, but we need at least one more session to address Stef's concern about your site, Claude—getting it to show up in the index. And consequently getting some traffic to the site. It's a bit of a black art, but it's an interesting topic."

Starting

Content

Design

AdSense

section five   **Traffic**

chapter nine

Making Money from Your Site

> Eric: Stef, are you still making money?

> Stef: Yes, though not a lot more than before.

> Claude: Well, I'm still not making any money and I don't think Anita is, either. It's disappointing.

> Eric: It's also pretty normal, Claude. You need to get traffic for your site. Remember, it's a numbers game—more traffic means more clicks.

> Claude: All right, then, what do I do—sorry, what do we do—to get more traffic?

> Eric: There's no magic bullet, but there are three basic approaches: Make it easy to find your site, spread the word about your site, and—this one will surprise you—advertise your site.

We met again a couple of weeks later, this time back at my house. Claude and Anita were publishing ads on their sites now, and Stef had done some tweaking of her AdSense code.

"I replaced the four-ad tower with a two-ad tower and an ad links unit," Stef was telling me as we sat down, "so now the ads take up a bit less space. Sometimes my blog entries are pretty short, and I didn't like the way the taller ads looked in that case."

"Are you still making money?" I asked her.

"Yes," she said, "though not a lot more than before."

"Well, I'm still not making any money," Claude said, "and I don't think Anita is, either." Anita shook her head. "It's disappointing."

"It's also pretty normal, Claude," I said. "How many page impressions per day are you seeing in the AdSense console?"

"I don't remember exactly, maybe 50 on average," Claude answered.

"Less than that for me," Anita said.

"And I bet some, if not all, of those impressions are from you visiting your own sites," I said. "That's the problem—you need to get traffic for your site. Remember, it's a numbers game—more traffic means more clicks. If your clickthrough rate is going to average 2 percent, for example, that means that you need at least 50 impressions to get one click."

"But I have 50 impressions a day," Claude protested.

"He means 50 impressions from *other* people, Dad," Stef explained.

"Stef's right, Claude," I continued, "you *can't* click ads on your own site, so your impressions are effectively meaningless. There's no way to distinguish your impressions from anyone else's in the AdSense console, but you need to account for them when viewing the reports. Anyhow, if you get enough traffic this isn't a problem—your own impressions won't make a big difference in the clickthrough rate."

"All right, then," he said, "what do I do—sorry, what do *we* do—to get more traffic?"

"There's no magic bullet," I said, "but there are three basic approaches: Make it easy to find your site, spread the word about your site, and—this one will surprise you—advertise your site."

"Advertise?" Anita asked. "You mean *buying* ads? I thought we were *showing* ads."

"You are," I said, "but sometimes it pays to advertise, so to speak. We'll get to that later, but let's start with the most important approach: making it easy to find your site."

Making It Easy to Find Your Site

"That's funny," Stef said, "I would have thought that word of mouth was the most important thing."

"No," Anita said, contradicting her sister, "I think making a site findable is more important. I have bookmarks for the sites I often visit, but there aren't that many of those. Most of the time, I just start the browser and Google for what I want."

"Ah yes," I said, "the newest verb in the English language: 'to Google.' I'm sure Google's lawyers have daily fits over that use of their trademark. But it underscores what Anita just said: People turn to search engines to find the information they want. If your site's not listed in the search engines, or it has a poor ranking, you'll miss out on a lot of traffic."

"Is it easy to get listed?" Claude asked.

"For the most part, yes," I said, "though it may take a while. The harder part is getting a *good* listing."

"You mean a high ranking?" he said.

"Yes," I explained, "the nearer you are to the top of a search-results page, the more traffic you'll get. A lot of Web site owners spend a lot of time trying to get their sites to rank higher in the listings. And to get their pages associated with the right keywords. They call the whole process *search engine optimization*, or SEO for short."

"Sounds scary," Anita said.

"Ah, it's just geek talk for getting better page rankings," I said. "The basics are pretty simple, and you've already done some of them: You've chosen good domain names; you've written good page titles and descriptions; you've put up relevant and keyword-rich content. Now it's a matter of spending time to get your sites *in* the search engines and then to bump up their rankings. Let's see how that's done." And I explained to them what search engine optimization is all about.

Getting Listed

The first step is to get listed in your favorite search engines. There are three ways to do this:

▶ Submit your Web address directly to the search engine for free.

▶ Get someone already listed to link to your site.

▶ Pay to have your site listed on one or more search engines.

Which you do depends entirely on the search engine you're targeting. Obviously, the free option appeals to most people. To submit a site to Google, fill out the simple form at `www.google.com/addurl` (**Figure 9.1**). To submit a site to Yahoo!, go to `submit.search.yahoo.com/free/request` (**Figure 9.2**)—you'll need to register for a Yahoo! account if you don't already have one. To submit to MSN Search, use the form at `search.msn.com/docs/submit.aspx` (**Figure 9.3**). Submitting your site to the major search engines only takes a few minutes and is well worth the effort.

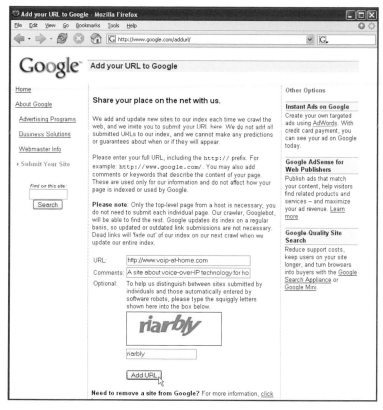

Figure 9.1 Submitting a site to Google.

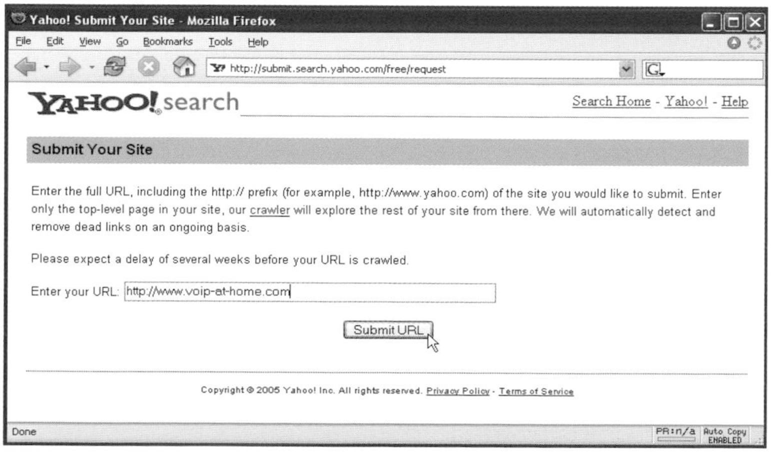

More Site Submissions

For the URL submission forms and guidelines for other sites, see the list of links at www.memwg. com/free-site-submit.

Figure 9.2 Submitting a site to Yahoo!

Downsides of Free Site Submission

Don't expect your site to show up immediately in the search engine's listings. It may take weeks before the search engine crawls (that is, inventories the pages of) your site. Or it may refuse your site for various reasons.

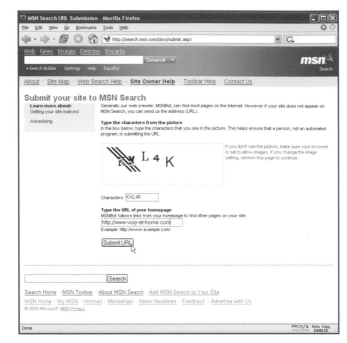

Figure 9.3 Submitting a site to MSN.

Not all search engines let you submit sites for free. Some require either a one-time payment or a subscription in order to list your site. There may be different payment levels available, with the pricier levels guaranteeing more prominent placement of your site in the search engine's results. Some sites, like Yahoo! and MSN, offer both free *and* paid submission options.

No Paid Submissions for Google

Google does not offer the option to pay to have your site listed in its index. All site submissions are free of charge. Site owners cannot pay to increase their page rankings: Google has always said that sponsored results (AdWords) do not affect how they rank pages relative to one another.

Is it worth paying for getting listed? Not initially. Submit your site to the search engines using their free submission forms as soon as you have a few good pages of content available, and spend your time (and money) working on other aspects of the site. Wait until the site's been running for a while and you've explored other avenues for increasing traffic.

The other way to be listed by a search engine is to get an already indexed site to link to yours. Search engines periodically recrawl the sites in their indexes, looking for new content and new links. If one of these sites links to a page on your site, the crawler will eventually find its way to that page. And if you've followed the linking rules laid out in Chapter 5, the search engine will then be able to find your site's home page and site map, and soon all your pages will find their way into the index.

The trick, of course, is to get a link to your site on someone else's site. If you know someone who already has an indexed site up and running, you can simply ask that person to link to your site. Getting your site mentioned in someone's blog is an easy way to do it if your site has useful information that the blogger thinks would be of interest to his or her readers. Note that the quality of the links to your site is also important—more on this shortly.

Getting listed in a Web directory—like the original Yahoo! directory (**Figure 9.4**) or the Google directory (**Figure 9.5**)—is another way to get into search engine indexes. (A directory is something like a phone book for Web sites.) For submissions to the Yahoo! directory, see the links near the bottom of the **http://search.yahoo.com/info/submit.html** page. The Google directory is actually based on the directory maintained by the Open Directory Project, also known as DMOZ or ODP, a Web-community effort. Getting listed is free, but it's a more involved (and sometimes controversial) process—see **http://dmoz.org/add.html** for more details.

Free Listing for Your Site

Purchasers of this book can apply to get their site listed for free on the www.memwg.com Web site if the site was built with the help of this book. See the full list of conditions at www.memwg.com/free-listing.

Figure 9.4 The Yahoo! directory.

Figure 9.5 The Google directory.

Determining Your Ranking

Each search engine arranges its search results in some manner. Complicated algorithms are used to determine which Web pages best match a given set of search terms. Search engine staff spend a lot of time tuning the algorithms in order to return the most relevant results possible to all kinds of queries. Even though the search service itself is free, it's all about making money: The better the results, the more the search engine is used; the more the search engine is used, the more money the search engine company makes by selling related services.

You don't just want your site to be listed by a search engine; you want your pages to rank high in the search results. Being ranked in the top ten sites for a given keyword is a surefire way to generate traffic for your site, especially if you can nab the first or second spot on the list. Of course, every other site owner wants the same thing, so you'll face stiff competition to get one of those prized rankings.

The PageRank Formula

The PageRank formula was created by Google founders Larry Page and Sergey Brin while they were Ph.D. students at Stanford University. The relative importance of a particular page is calculated according to the number of other pages that link to it and how important those other pages are themselves. A basic description of the formula is found on the Google Web site at `www.google.com/technology`, but see the list at `www.memwg.com/pagerank` for more details about the formula.

How search engines rank individual pages is a matter of great debate among Web site owners. For competitive reasons, search engines rarely disclose more than vague details about their page-ranking algorithms. Even the famous PageRank formula—the one that

PageRank Tools

Firefox and Mozilla users can download an open-source browser extension that displays the current page's PageRank in the browser's status bar. See www.memwg.com/ pagerank for details.

determines a site's popularity by counting the number of other sites that link to it—is just a small (though important) part of Google's ranking algorithm.

Competition isn't the only reason search engines keep their algorithms proprietary. Once key algorithms like the PageRank formula are generally known, site owners start to adapt their pages specifically for the algorithms in order to favorably skew the search engine results their way. For example, *link farms*—groups of Web sites created specifically to increase the number of links to targeted pages—were used early on to bump up Google page rankings. Search engines are constantly monitoring and adjusting their search algorithms in order to avoid this kind of overt manipulation.

The simplest way to determine a page's ranking is to search using page-related keywords and see where the page ends up in the search results. Since your site is keyword-driven itself (to display more relevant ads), this should yield fairly accurate results.

Another way to determine page ranking is to use Google's Toolbar (**Figure 9.6**). The Toolbar, currently available only for Internet Explorer, can display a page's relative PageRank on a scale from 0 to 10, with 10 being the most important and 0 the least. The higher the PageRank, the higher your page's ranking within a search.

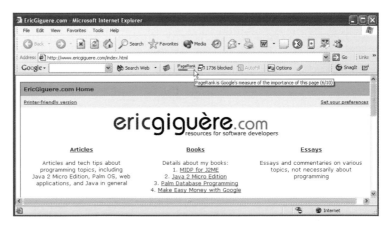

Figure 9.6 Determining PageRank with the Google Toolbar.

Improving Your Ranking

As long as you're not doing it deceptively or fraudulently, there's nothing wrong with trying to improve your site's search engine rankings. This is what search engine optimization (SEO) is all about.

There are two basic techniques for improving a page's ranking. The first is to ensure that the page has good content and good keyword density. This should be a no-brainer—you should already be creating your pages this way if you want AdSense to display relevant ads. Watch for missing keywords, though—try to figure out what people are really searching for and make sure your page gets included in the search results.

The other technique is to get highly ranked pages to link to your page. This increases the relative importance of your own page, especially if the anchor text of the link (the text that the user clicks to activate the link) contains keywords relevant to your site. While this technique works especially well with Google, where the popularity of a page is a fundamental part of the PageRank formula, all search engines use incoming links as an important ranking tool. Note that the reverse can also be true: Incoming links from poorly ranked pages—especially those that have been removed from search engine indexes due to overt attempts at page-rank manipulation—will drag down the page's ranking.

As you might imagine, obtaining high-quality incoming links to your site can be a challenge. You can try to initiate a *link swap* with the other site, whereby you both agree to link to each other's sites— the classic "you scratch my back and I'll scratch yours" situation. But link swaps only work if both parties feel they have something to gain from the relationship.

Of course, if you have unique, useful content, other sites will start linking to yours without any prompting on your part. This can be a mixed blessing, however, because you have no control over the quality of those incoming links.

Do You Crawl Here Often?

Improving your site's search engine rankings is a slow process because it depends on how often search engines crawl your site, and that may happen as seldom as every few weeks— there's no set schedule.

Spreading the Word About Your Site

"So getting a good ranking is a slow process," Claude said, disappointed. "That's too bad."

"Well, if it were truly easy, everyone would be doing it," I said, "and nothing would be any different anyhow. Watch out for scam artists who'll promise you high rankings in exchange for a hefty fee. A quality search engine optimization consultant won't promise overnight results. You have to think long-term."

"What about the short term, then?" Stef asked. "Can you do anything to get more traffic while you're working toward a higher page ranking?"

"Sure you can," I said, "by spreading the word about your site."

"You mean publicizing it," Anita said.

"Yes," I agreed, "but not as formally as you might think. Actually, the term that's in vogue these days for what I'm about to describe is *viral marketing*."

"Viral? As in infections?" Claude asked.

"Exactly," I continued, "but without the negative connotations. The basic idea of viral networking is to use word-of-mouth recommendations and subtle or subliminal mentions to get people to visit your site."

"But why is it called *viral*?" Claude asked. "I still don't understand."

"I know," said Stef, "it's because the Internet makes it easy to spread the word about something. Like in a blog posting. Or by sending an instant message to your friends."

"You're absolutely right, Stef," I agreed, "the basic premise of viral marketing is to create a self-perpetuating buzz about a product or service. Get a few key people recommending your product and they'll tell their friends, who'll tell others, and so on."

"I've read about this before," Anita said. "Viral marketing is used to promote new pop stars, to get a buzz about them going in the chat rooms."

"Well, I'm not suggesting you hire people to flog your site in chat rooms," I said, "but there are some simple things you can do to get the word out."

Embed Web Addresses

A simple but effective technique is to embed your site's Web address in all your outgoing mail messages and forum postings. The easiest way to do this is by setting up a *signature*. A signature is a brief message (keep it between one and four lines) that is automatically appended to your messages or postings. For example, Claude might send an email like this:

```
Dear John:

Thanks for the email, I'm glad you liked the movie. We
really enjoyed it, too. Talk to you soon!

Claude
My site about Internet phoning—http://www.VoIP-at-Home.com
```

The last two lines of this message are the signature. It's usually stored in a separate text file (**Figure 9.7**). You then adjust your email application's options to append the signature file to outgoing messages (**Figure 9.8**). You do a similar thing with online forums and chat rooms, embedding Web addresses in your signatures and/or profiles.

Figure 9.7 Creating a signature file.

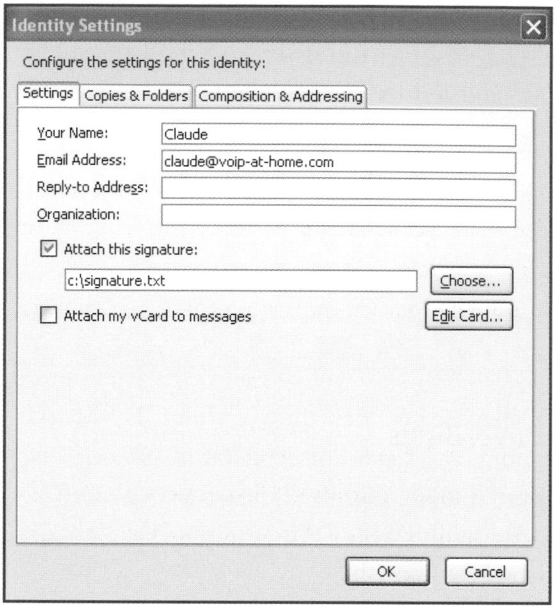

Figure 9.8 Automatically appending a signature to outgoing mail.

Be sure to add the "http://" prefix to the Web address. Most mail readers use that as a cue to automatically transform the address into a link that the reader can click to jump directly to the Web site.

Be discreet when using signatures, and keep them short. If you've chosen a good domain name, you shouldn't need more than a line or two to mention it.

Create or Write for Newsletters

Once you develop expertise in a subject, consider either creating your own newsletter or writing articles for other newsletters. Newsletters are somewhat old-fashioned, but they're easily forwarded from one person to another and can be printed out for later reading as well.

Creating a newsletter is actually a lot of work, especially if you intend to publish it on a frequent schedule. You'll need mailing-list management software to maintain the subscriber list. Your Web hosting provider can often create a mailing list for you. The hard part is coming up with good content on a regular basis. Be sure to promote your Web site in the newsletter.

Writing for other newsletters is simpler, especially if you're not expecting to be paid for your work. Mention your site in the author biography at the end of the article—if people like what you said, they'll probably visit your site to learn more about you and/or the topic.

Use (But Don't Abuse) Blogs

In some ways, blogs are the modern form of newsletters. If your site isn't itself a blog, consider adding a blog. You can do what Stef does and use a free blogging service like Blogger. Or your Web hosting provider may be able to add one to your site for you.

Once your blog is up and running, add an entry to it whenever you make a significant change or addition to the site. This lets people know what's happening on the site—it's another form of a "what's new" page. Add entries referring to news items related to your site's topic, things that otherwise wouldn't make it onto your site. It's another way to add content to your site (and don't forget to show ads!).

Search for other blogs that are related to your site and look for opportunities to comment on other people's blog entries. Do this only when you have something interesting or substantial to say; otherwise you'll be accused of *comment spam*—making spurious comments simply to promote your own site—and banned from making further comments.

Cross-Promote Your Sites

Once you have two or more sites going, be sure to cross-promote them by having them link to each other. You could do this on the about pages or by including them in the footers of certain pages.

Ad Newsletter

Martin Lemieux's SmartAds newsletter (www.smartads.info/ncwsletter/) is an interesting example of a newsletter devoted specifically to Web ad trends.

Spam Ban Plan

Google has a plan to ban comment spam. See www.google.com/googleblog/2005/01/preventing-comment-spam.html.

Advertising Your Site

"Shouldn't you also pursue traditional promotional opportunities?" Anita said.

"Such as?" I asked.

"Such as getting profiled in the local newspaper or getting a radio interview."

"Absolutely," I said. "Everything helps. But those things rarely happen for niche topics—newspapers and radio stations want topics that interest a broad cross-section of their audience. Still, it's certainly worth a try once your site's established."

"You mentioned one other thing—advertising your site," said Claude, "which sounded kind of bizarre to me. The costs would just eat into your profits."

"Not if you do it right," I said. "The key is to make more money from the extra traffic than you're paying to get the traffic. As long as you do that, you'll be ahead."

"So you want us to sign up for AdWords?" Stef asked.

"Not necessarily," I answered. "AdWords is the obvious choice, yes, and you already know how it works thanks to our previous session on keyword valuation. In fact, we even went as far as setting up a fake ad campaign—remember that?" They all nodded. "But AdWords isn't the only choice. You can sign up for link-exchange programs. You can buy banner ads. Don't worry—there are lots of ways to spend your advertising budget! I'd start with AdWords, though. It's a proven advertising vehicle—Stef's already benefiting from it, after all—and it doesn't cost much to try out."

"But how likely is it that we'll make more money from buying ads that are similar to the ones we're already showing?" Claude said. "Wouldn't they cost us the same or even more?"

"Probably," I admitted. "It depends on what you're trying to accomplish. If you just want to build awareness and get some more eyeballs viewing your site, something like AdWords works well. If you want to generate direct revenue from the ads, you need to do one of two things: either use low-cost keywords to target pages with high-paying keywords, or use affiliate and referral programs that pay you money whenever someone buys a product or service because of you."

Tracking Visitors to Your Site

"Well, I'm willing to try it out," Claude said. "It sounds easy enough to do."

"It is," I said, "but it brings up an important topic—tracking where your visitors are coming from. If you're spending money to get traffic, you want to know if you're wasting your money or not!"

Tracking Visitors with Referrer Headers

When you click a link, the browser contacts the Web server specified in the link and requests the appropriate page. The browser sends extra information along with the request. One of those pieces of information is known as the *referrer header*, which tells the Web server how the browser was referred to the page.

Suppose, for example, that a visitor to the page www.ericgiguere.com/index.html clicks that page's link to www.memwg.com/index.html. As part of the the page-fetch request, the Web server hosting www.memwg.com gets a referrer header that looks like this:

```
Referer: http://www.ericgiguere.com/index.html
```

(The word "referer" is misspelled deliberately, for historical reasons.) Now, the browser is not required to send the Referer header when it requests a page. Some users disable the header for privacy reasons, but most browsers send them quite routinely.

Tracking referrers is a great way to find out more about how visitors arrive at your site. You can tell when someone finds your site with Google, for example, because the referrer header starts with "`http://www.google.com`." Usually, you can even tell what keywords they used to find you. Consider the following referrer header as an example:

```
Referer: http://www.google.com/search?num=
100&q=voip+long+distance
```

This header tells you that the visitor found your page with the search terms *voip long distance* (spaces are represented by plus signs). This kind of information can help you fine-tune your pages and can even suggest new keywords and topics for your site.

Ask your Web hosting service how to track referrer information—it varies from system to system.

Tracking Visitors with Landing Pages

Referrer headers aren't the only way to track visitors. Advertising campaigns can also use special-purpose *landing pages* for tracking clicks. You create a separate landing page for each of your advertisements. The landing pages have no content; all they do is redirect the browser to another page on the site. Each time someone clicks one of your ads, the visitor gets sent to the appropriate landing page before being redirected to the actual destination page.

For the visitor, it's just as if the browser went directly to the destination page, but you've actually gathered a valuable piece of information: *exactly which ad brought the visitor to your site*. By examining your Web server's access logs—files that record browser page requests—you can quickly determine which ads are working well and which aren't.

An alternative to creating landing pages is to embed a unique identifier into the Web address (the URL) used in the ad link. Just add a question mark to the end of the URL and a name-value pair like "from=ad1." (This is called a *query parameter*.) In other words, instead of using this URL:

```
http://www.voip-at-home.com/index.html
```

use the following URL for one ad:

```
http://www.voip-at-home.com/index.html?from=ad1
```

and this URL for a second ad:

```
http://www.voip-at-home.com/index.html?from=ad2
```

You can easily pick these out from the Web server's access logs.

The great thing about landing pages and query parameters is that they work even if referrer headers are disabled.

It Takes Time

"The important thing to remember about these approaches, however," I said, "is that they take time to be effective. Your sites are up, but your work isn't over—you'll need to keep working on them."

"But you don't have to spend a *lot* of time, do you?" Anita asked. "It's been hard to find the time to build my site. I was looking forward to taking a break."

"It depends on what your goals are for the site," I answered. "You can certainly let it coast for a while. If your costs are minimal and the site's bringing in more than you're spending on it, you can afford to work on something else."

"Like another site!" Claude laughed.

"Yeah, or maybe some extra sleep," I suggested. "Anyhow, just be patient and work at it." I leaned back in my chair. "I think we're pretty much done now. Feel free to call me with any questions, but there's not much more to tell you other than wishing you good luck with your ventures. And be sure to let me know how things are going."

chapter ten

Expanding Your Horizons

> **Eric:** So, how's it been going? I've been peeking at your site every once in a while. You've done a great job at filling it with content.

> **Claude:** It's actually going pretty good. I'm definitely into the updating stage, I'm pretty sure I have enough content right now to keep visitors happy.

> **Eric:** So what are you going to do now? Let the site coast and the money roll in?

> **Claude:** I wish! There's a lot of competition for the voice-over-IP stuff, so I won't be buying a house in Bermuda anytime soon. But I *am* making money, which is great. And I *have* been looking at some other things. You mentioned affiliate and referral programs and I got curious about them so I did some research and what I found out was surprising.

Claude and I met for lunch a few weeks later. I wanted to catch up on what he and his daughters had been up, but we didn't need our computers for that.

"So," I began, after placing the food order, "how's it been going? I've been peeking at your site every once in a while. You've done a great job at filling it with content."

"It's actually going pretty good," Claude said. "I'm definitely into the updating stage, I'm pretty sure I have enough content right now to keep visitors happy. Stef's also happy with her blog."

"Yeah, I can tell," I said, "I've been reading it on occasion. She's even talked about the process she went through to put up the ads and how easy it was." I laughed. "She's become an AdSense expert!"

"Yeah," he said, "she's definitely enthusiastic about it. Mind you, she's enthusiastic about everything she writes about in her blog. *Too* enthusiastic about some things, to my mind."

"Oh, don't be such a grumpy father," I said, "I'm sure if you were her age you'd be writing things your parents didn't approve of. How's Anita doing?"

"Well," he began, "obviously she doesn't have as much time as I do to work on her Web site. But I think it's coming along well. She's not out to make a lot of money either, so her goals are different."

"So what are you going to do now?" I asked him. "Let the site coast and the money roll in?"

He laughed. "Hah! I wish," he said. "There's a lot of competition for the voice-over-IP stuff out there, so I won't be buying a house in Bermuda anytime soon. But I *am* making money, which is great. I just can't retire from it."

"But you *are* retired," I protested.

"You know what I mean," he said.

"Claude," I continued, "now that you've been bitten by the AdSense bug, you've discovered you have an entrepreneurial side you never knew you had. Am I right?"

"Well," he said, somewhat sheepishly, "you're probably right. I *have* been looking at some other things."

"Setting up another site?" I asked.

"That," he admitted, "but other things, too. You mentioned affiliate and referral programs in our last group session and I got curious about them."

"Really?" I said. "So what did you do?"

"I did some research," he continued, "and what I found out was surprising. Did you know there are people out there who buy AdWords ads and don't actually sell *anything*? All they do is refer people to other sites and make money when *those* people buy something."

"That's right," I agreed, "it's strictly a numbers game again. If an ad costs you ten cents per click and you get five dollars every time someone buys the product or service you're referring, you come out ahead if at least two out of every fifty clicks leads to a sale."

"Yeah, and some people claim to do quite well at it," he said, "but it's kind of risky for me. You can spend a lot of money and not make anything at all. No, I'm not ready for that just yet! But I *did* sign up for Amazon's affiliate program."

"For the books, I take it?"

"Yeah," he said, "since I already had a list of recommended books on my site, it was a natural fit. Now, if anyone buys a book—or almost anything else—on Amazon because of me, Amazon pays me a commission."

"Was it hard to do?" I asked him.

"Hard? No. If you have a Web site already, it's easy to do. Here, let me tell you all about it." And he did.

But that's another story.

Index

advertisements. *See* ads
advertising, 6–7. *See also* marketing; Web
  advertising
AdWords
  ad selection, 38–39
  image ads, 38
  keywords, 66–69
  overview, 36–38, 240–241
  text ads, 37–38
aggregate data, 184–187
Amazon Honor System program, 25
Amazon.com, 26, 247

B

Back button, 127, 213
backgrounds, 136, 163–164
backup services, 110
bandwidth, 84, 108
banner ads, 27–29, 40, 207
Blogger service, 18–19
blogging services, 18–19, 82, 169, 239
blogs. *See also* Web sites
  ads in, 20, 196
  basics, 18
  control of, 82–84
  described, 18, 57
  making money from, 18–20
  motivation for, 57, 60
  as promotional tool, 239
  publishing on Web site, 169–171
  templates for, 132
  vs. Web sites, 18
book recommendations, 247
Brin, Sergey, 233
browsers
  alternative, 138
  color display on, 137, 162
  launching, 157–158
  listing page ranking in, 234
  page display in, 152
  pop-up ads, 20, 28
  redirecting, 219
  support for, 138

C

cascading style sheets (CSS), 160
channel data, 184–187
Channel section, 211
channel tracking, 43–44
channels
  custom, 43–44, 184–189, 211
  tracking performance with, 220
  URL, 44, 184–187, 220–221

click fraud, 32–33, 36, 59, 205
click tracking, 31–32. *See also* pay-per-click
  advertising
ClickZ Network, 26–27
code. *See* AdSense code; HTML
color
  alternate ads, 209–210
  on Web, 137, 161–162
  Web pages, 136–137
color palettes, 42, 199, 209
color schemes, 42, 198–200, 209
comment spam, 239
competition, 70
content, 55–80
  changes to, 8
  copyright issues, 77–79
  creating, 9, 70–79
  grammar/spelling, 75–76
  importance of, 6
  quality standards, 6, 49–50
  restrictions on, 48–49
  showcasing on Web site, 132–139
context, 23, 130–132
cookies, 31
copyright/trademark issues, 77–79, 94, 135, 227
crawlers, 30, 63, 218, 221, 231
CSS (cascading style sheets), 160
CSS editor, 160, 164, 166
customer support, 49, 183

D

database services, 110
design. *See* Web site design
disk space, 108
DNS (Domain Name System), 85–86, 89
domain name registrars, 89–90, 97–98, 101
Domain Name System (DNS), 85–86, 89
domain names, 84–103
  described, 17, 85–86
  email addresses, 102
  expiration/renewal of, 90
  hijacked, 103
  multiple, 96
  obtaining, 18, 84, 92–101
  purchasing, 84, 101
  registering, 92, 101–103
  rules for, 86
domains
  international, 86–87, 96
  locked, 103
  names. *See* domain names
  searching for, 98–101
  subdomains, 87–89
  top-level (TLD), 86–90, 95–98

E

elevator pitch, 4–5
email
    aliases, 109–110
    sending, 109
    signatures, 237–238
    spam, 12, 90, 110, 112, 239
email addresses
    adding links for, 155–157
    domain names, 102
email services
    free email clients, 102, 109
    permanent, 102
    Web hosting plans, 104, 109–110
EricGiguere.com Web site, 4–5, 17
Error pages, 213

F

fame, 58
Fastclick, 30
file transfer protocol. *See* FTP
finding. *See* searching
fonts, 135–136, 162–163
fortune, 58–59
forums, 110
Framed pages section, 211
frames, 211
FTP (file transfer protocol), 153
FTP services, 110, 169–170

G

Google
    making money with, 3–20
    page rankings, 8–9, 227–228, 232–235
    submitting sites to, 228–232
Google AdSense. *See* AdSense
Google AdWords. *See* AdWords
Google directory, 231–232
Google home page, 120–124
Google search box, 214–218
Google Toolbar, 22, 46, 234
grammar, 75–76

H

headings, 131
home page, 120–124, 127
host name, 17
hosting services, 17, 104–112
HTML. *See also* AdSense code
    learning about, 151
    overview, 15, 141–143
    viewing raw, 147, 150, 214

HTML tags, 151, 161
HTTP address, 153

I

image ads, 28, 38, 40
images, 39, 76
indexes, search engine, 221, 230–231, 235
Internet. *See also* Web
    costs related to, 24–25
    described, 23–24
    privacy issues, 58, 90–91, 101, 242
    usage statistics, 6
    vs. Web, 23–24
interstitials, 28
IP addresses, 85, 88–89, 96, 102–103, 111

J

JavaScript, 34–35, 203

K

keyword values, 63–65
keywords
    ad selection, 38–39
    AdWords. *See* AdWords
    high-paying, 69–70
    listing for sites, 93–94
    text ads, 37
    tips for, 131

L

landing pages, 127, 242–243
languages, 149, 190, 214–215
leaderboard, 40
licenses, 79
link farms, 234
link swaps, 235
links
    ad, 28–29, 37–38, 40
    broken, 157
    creating with Nvu, 155–157
    email, 155–157
    external, 130
    inline, 130
    navigation, 127–130
    sponsored, 28–29, 37
    to Web pages, 8, 127–130
LiveJournal service, 18–19
locators, 131–132

M

mailing lists, 110

making money, 225–244. *See also* payments
    from blogging, 18–20
    example of, 10–14
    with Google, 3–20
    as motivator, 58–59, 61
    overview, 4–9
margins, 141–142, 164
marketing. *See also* advertising
    elevator pitch, 4–5
    viral, 236–237
markup language, 142–143
meta tag, 219
Metaspy, 63
money. *See* making money
motivation, 57–61
MSN Search, 228, 230
My Accounts tab, 190–193

N

name servers, 102–103
navigation, 127–130
navigation bar, 129, 132, 134
newsletters, as promotional tool, 238–239
nonprofits, 59–60
Nvu application, 15, 144–158

O

Overture. *See* Yahoo! Search Marketing

P

Page, Larry, 233
PageRank formula, 233–235
passwords, 178
pay-per-click advertising
    click fraud, 32–33, 36, 59, 205
    overview, 7, 31–32
    rates, 13, 37, 60, 65, 69
payments, 193–194. *See also* making money
    account settings, 190–193
    detailed reporting of, 44
    direct deposit, 193–194
    frequency of, 44–45, 193
    history, 190–191
    hold on, 190
    monthly, 44–45
    overview, 193–194
    tax information, 192–193
    viewing, 178–179
PayPal, 25, 119
performance
    ad, 178, 184, 220
    reports for, 184–187
    tracking with channels, 220

philanthropy, 59–60
pixels, 198
plagiarism, 77–79
pop-under ads, 28
pop-up ads, 20, 28
portal, 122–123
Preview Tool, 180–182
previews
    ads, 180–182
    Web pages, 157–158
printing Web pages, 136–137, 160
privacy considerations, 58, 90–91, 101, 242
profits. *See* making money; payments
proxy servers, 30
public domain, 78
public-service announcements (PSAs), 43, 203, 210
publisher ID, 34
publisher management console, 35–38, 177–192, 211–214
publishers. *See* AdSense publishers
publishing. *See* Web publishing

Q

query parameter, 243

R

rankings, 8–9, 227–228, 232–235
referrer headers, 241–242
registrars, 89–90, 97–98, 101
registry, 87
reports, 44, 178–179, 184–187
Reports tab, 184–187
research, general, 62

S

scams, avoiding, 178, 236
script services, 110
search boxes, 128, 214–218
search code, adding, 214–218
search engine indexes, 221, 230–231, 235
search engine optimization (SEO), 228–232
search engines
    domains, 98–101
    free submissions, 228, 230
    getting listed in, 228–232
    Google. *See* Google
    mining for ideas, 62–63
    MSN Search, 228, 230
    rankings, 8–9, 227–228, 232–235
    site maps and, 128
    submitting sites to, 228–232
    Yahoo!, 63–65, 228–230